Winning Is A Science And Art

How To Increase The Odds Of Victory, Win Any Argument You Desire And Unleash Your Inner Champion

HALBERT WARD

© Copyright 2024 - All rights reserved.

The content inside this book may not be duplicated, reproduced, or transmitted without direct written permission from the author or publisher.

Under no circumstances will any blame or legal responsibility be held against the publisher, or author, for any damages, reparation, or monetary loss due to the information contained within this book, either directly or indirectly.

Legal Notice:

This book is copyright protected. It is only for personal use. You cannot amend, distribute, sell, use, quote or paraphrase any part, or the content within this book, without the consent of the author or publisher.

Disclaimer Notice:

Please note the information contained within this document is for educational and entertainment purposes only. All effort has been executed to present accurate, reliable, up to date, complete information. No warranties of any kind are declared or implied. Readers acknowledge that the author is not engaging in the rendering of legal, financial, medical, or professional advice. The content within this book has been derived from various sources. Please consult a licensed professional before attempting any techniques outlined in this book.

By reading this document, the reader agrees that under no circumstances is the author responsible for any losses, direct or indirect, that are incurred as a result of the use of the information contained within this document, including, but not limited to, errors, omissions, or inaccuracies.

TABLE OF CONTENT

INTRODUCTION

Every one of us has experienced the challenge of convincing other individuals at one time or the other, whether we are trying to convince a colleague about something important or trying to win an argument with someone. Understanding the science and art of winning will increase your chances of victory, instead of simply relying on your instinct alone and making mistakes or not achieving success. This book shares powerful techniques that will help you become a winner in life.

Are you stuck in a place and feeling uncertain about your future? Do you want to accomplish great things but don't know how to tap into your full potential? The chapters of this book will guide and show you how to believe in yourself and succeed in life. It will help you unleash your inner champion.

What thought would come to your mind if you were told that you possess the untapped potential for a winner's mindset? What would you think if you were told that this potential is waiting to be unleashed so that you can accomplish great things? Unleashing the unstoppable force within you, which is your winner's mindset will propel you toward greatness.

In this book, we uncover the truth any individual who wants to be a champion or a winner needs to know and the strategies they can use to tap into their inner champion, develop the confidence they need, and achieve great results.

So, whether you desire personal growth, success in your relationships, or advancement in your career, this book will empower you with the insights and tools to get in the driver's seat of your life and become the champion. You will learn the exact tactics needed to unleash your inner champion and conquer the world. You just need to be confident and continue pushing yourself to move ahead no matter the situation. There is no giving up.

This book is a roadmap to becoming the best of you. It all begins with believing in yourself. Belief is the foundation for unleashing the champion within. You must have faith in your vision and believe in yourself. You must also believe that with perseverance and hard work, your dream can become a reality. You must believe in your abilities even when you are going through challenges and other individuals doubt your abilities. But belief in yourself alone is not all you need. You need to take the necessary action and be ready to make the sacrifices that are necessary to accomplish your goals.

This book is your guide to taking the right action, staying true to your purpose, surrounding yourself with positivity, and being resilient. This journey requires dedication and hard work, but you will receive many rewards. You will learn to recognize the unique abilities and talents you have and how to tap into your potential. You will also learn how to find the courage to pursue your dreams, even when you are experiencing setbacks and challenges, and learn to never give up no matter how hard the journey may be.

Do you feel in control of your life? Do you feel like everything is already decided for you, or that you can make changes whenever you want?

Don't leave yourself at the mercy of fate, getting tossed around by the universe, and living a life that is completely out of your control.

Are you the type who believes you cannot consciously choose to achieve success? You can have whatever you want, whether it be money, relationships, or jobs.

You are working hard but still find yourself frustrated and hoping that the solution to your situation will magically appear out of nowhere. But things don't always happen magically.

So, how can you turn things around?

When you master your ability to manifest what you want, things will begin to change for the better.

Manifesting means bringing your goals or dreams to reality. Learning how to focus and direct your attention on the positive things you want to see in your life can make you feel in control of your life. Anyone can consciously create success, and that includes you. But before you can do this, you need to get rid of negative energy and fill yourself with positive energy. What this means is dealing with any issues that have lasted for too long, and you can even see a therapist or counselor if you need to.

Once this foundation has been built, you have the focus and energy to consciously create the kind of life you desire. If you don't deal with these issues, you will have too much stuff holding you back.

What if you were able to control what happens in your life? What if you could choose every detail of the events? What if you could just choose where you wanted to be?

All the choices in life are spread out before you and you can choose which direction you want to lead your life in. You may be fed up with your current life situation and craving success. However, it is not the end of your story. You can still travel the world, own luxury cars and houses, and get all the good things you desire. You just need to be deliberate about creating the life you desire, and visualization can usher you into this reality. This book shows you all you need to win.

CHAPTER ONE
The Science Of Winning

Every one of us wants to achieve success in our lives. Nobody wants to get to the end of their lives and discover that they cannot reflect on goals achieved and a life well lived. But success doesn't mean the same thing to everyone. It means different things to different people. For some individuals, success may mean working for a big organization and earning a big salary. For some others, it may mean being there for their family and spending quality time with them. For you, it may mean making a change in the world by inspiring people to be the change themselves.

Although there is a science and an art to winning, you need to first understand what success means to you. If you don't clearly understand this and your destination, you will never get to your destination even if you keep following the process to get there. So, take some minutes to think about what you want to achieve and write down what success means to you.

You must have heard people talk about the science of winning or the art of winning, and we will discuss both science and art.

We cannot do without science. It defines the laws that govern our world and our lives, and these laws exist, whether you believe that they do or not. You don't have to believe that gravity exists before you feel or see its work in the world. You will definitely fall if you jump off a story building. You can't jump and find yourself going upwards; you will definitely go downwards. You can only control how you fall and this is where art is involved.

Falling may not be your choice, but once you lose your balance, science dictates that you have no control over the fall. However, you can control how you fall.

Everyone is subject to the laws that govern the planet. What you can control is the manner in which you use those laws. You need to first have a full understanding of the science that governs the lives of humans and then you can apply artful living.

Gravity is not the science I am talking about here. I am talking about our thoughts, words, and actions. Everything that has ever existed on this planet was first "thought". From being a thought, it became a conversion, and then actions were taken to create it. When you achieve the goal you want to achieve, you get there because you had a dream. When you have a dream, you start working towards that dream. You don't sit and wait for it to come to pass. If you have a business idea, start working on it. You can speak to a few people and launch the business. You think about something, speak about it, and then act. Growing a business requires that you think about it, speak about it, and take the necessary actions.

You need to understand that this is science. You may not be aware of what is going on, but everyone on this planet is subject to it and they use it, whether they believe it or not. In fact, most individuals don't know anything about the power that their thoughts and words have.

Your thoughts and words create the reality you experience. If you go through life believing that you are unworthy, things will be that way for you. What happens is that you will be quick to accept people's bad behaviors whenever they treat you unfairly. You have made up your mind to support your unworthiness by staying focused on evidence that supports the negative thoughts you have about yourself. I'm sure you remember some good times in your life. What about those times? Did you choose the times that good things happened to you as evidence to remind you that you are worthy to have the good things in life? I bet you didn't. You simply said, "Wow, this is a nice surprise." You are who you think you are. Your thoughts and words are creating your reality, whether you are aware of it or not. So, if you think you will win, you will speak the words and your actions will start corresponding with your words and thoughts.

If you have the desire to create a life worth living, you need to ask yourself how you will operate within these laws. Will you actively use them to create your desired reality? Or will you keep being unaware of how your destiny is being created by your thoughts and words?

Many people consider arguing to be something to stay away from. But arguments are not always bad; they can be used for good purposes. You can use arguments to challenge old ideas and also inform people of what you want them to know. Arguments also have the ability to sharpen the minds of people. We will look at strategies you can use to argue more incisively, which will help you win the discussion. Different people see winning in different ways. It means different things to them.

You find yourself in the middle of a heated argument and the individual you are arguing with appears unwilling to understand what you are telling them. What is the way forward?

You need to first understand that you can boost the other individual's receptiveness to your ideas by reframing your ideas.

The human brain has a limited ability to process information. So, it deploys frames as it is necessary. Your mind uses frames to help you store and interpret information. Although the brain is powerful, it creates categories that help it understand the world. How an individual sees and responds to what you do and say is determined by the type of frame the person is using. For example, if you are trying to buy a new car, you might look at it through three different frames. The first frame might be that the car is white, the second frame might be that the car costs $50,000, and the third frame might be that the car is one year old. Frame one is aesthetic, frame two is economic, and frame three is historical.

While we can have all this information in mind simultaneously, the frames can also be rearranged in order of preference. The frame you prefer will change the way you perceive the value of the car and influence whether or not you will buy the car.

So, how can you change frames and convince a person who is stuck in a particular frame to consider another frame? How can you convince them to see the validity of the argument you are making? You need to first reframe your own position if you want to change the person's frame.

Studies show that you will have a high success rate if you reframe your message to leverage your listener's existing beliefs. If you want to convince an individual and win them to your position, the best thing to do is to get your position connected to their beliefs and not challenge their beliefs. What this means is that you agree with values you may not necessarily share. It makes other individuals see your position's legitimacy, and the perceptual gap that exists between your viewpoint and their viewpoints is reduced.

So, if you find yourself arguing with a colleague who is not willing to continue a new project, you could say that you respect their commitment to doing what they believe is the best thing to do for the organization. "Can we discuss some reasons why this new project will help the organization?"

When you say this to the individual, you reframe the issue around something that you both believe in, which is the organization's health. You may be sharing a plan with your manager about making improvements to production rates and your manager then tells you that the idea you are recommending is a costly one. You can reframe your position by linking it to your manager's existing beliefs instead of trying to justify the high cost. You can say something like, it's a good thing that you want to improve our organization's production capabilities to help us meet the year's new objectives. I am concerned that our ability to grow our output will be limited if we under-invest in these upgrades, and this will cost us so much in lost production. I have come up with a plan to help us increase production so that our objectives will be met.

This shows that you need to understand the perspective of your opponent to win any argument. Once you understand their perspective, you can then connect the beliefs supporting your opponent's perspective to the argument you are making. You want to influence the individual and get them to your side by finding common ground. You don't want to stand on the opposite side and shout across the divide.

Every one of us has met people who seem to have little to no understanding of the events happening in the world but who are great at speaking with conviction and confidence.

Most people believe that they can explain things in great detail. However, if asked, they provide incoherent and vague explanations. The issue is that people usually confuse a little familiarity that they have with general concepts for in-depth knowledge.

Our knowledge is also highly selective. We easily forget what doesn't support our beliefs and remember facts that support those beliefs. It is pointless to simply ask why people oppose a policy or support it. It is important that you ask how a particular thing works to have an effect. Our critical thinking skills can also be affected by politics. According to research, if an argument's conclusion supports people's viewpoints, they don't notice the logical fallacies in the argument. However, if these people are shown contrary evidence, they will be more highly critical of the smallest hole in the argument. This is referred to as motivated reasoning.

We are not necessarily shielded from these flaws when we have a high standard of education. Having a high standard of education might make you overestimate your understanding of your degree subject. You might forget the details even though you remember the subject's general content. Individuals usually confuse the present level of understanding that they have with their peak knowledge. This is a false sense of expertise. This is the reason discussions that have to do with politics can leave you feeling like you are banging your head against a brick wall even when you are discussing with individuals you might otherwise respect. Fortunately, studies also offer evidence-based ways people can have more fruitful discussions.

Instead of asking why, you can ask how. Some political arguments are based on false premises, and even though the individual might have a minimal understanding of the situation at hand, they speak with great confidence. As a result of this, asking for more detail is a great way to deflate someone's argument. You need to make the other individual focus on how something would play itself out. A humbler attitude is prompted when you reveal the shallowness of the knowledge they presently have.

CHAPTER TWO
The Art Of Winning

We have seen the science of winning in the previous chapter. We will also dive into the art of winning. Art is as unique and individual as the patterns on your fingertips. It is up to you to apply this art the way you want to. However, you need to have an awareness of your thought patterns, or else, you will continue living your life with no real direction. You will only be living as a victim of circumstance with no control of your life and life will keep happening to you.

This art can be applied to your life in a variety of ways and you can use many different tools such as meditation, visualization, journalling, breathing exercises, mindfulness, and so on. The tools you use don't really matter. What matters is that you find the right ones that will help you win. Finding your art within the science will help you become everything you want to be.

You can kick-start the process by becoming aware of your words as they are in accordance with your thoughts. Ask family members and friends to alert you to the things that you say without thinking. They should draw your attention to what you say habitually. You might be repeatedly saying things are pretty tough, and things might even be tough for you in reality. Are you surprised about that? You shouldn't be because you have been speaking those words into your reality.

Once you get to know the things you say habitually, do a silent reflection on where they originate from, and look for something positive to use in replacing them. At this point, you just need to stop saying the negative things you say habitually that bring you trouble.

You need to pay attention to your actions because they actually speak louder than words. This is the truth. Become aware of your thoughts, words, and actions, and ask yourself if this is who you really want to be. If this is not who you want to be, change.

Don't forget that your foundation is your identity. As you create the life of your dreams, you need to see yourself in a positive way. How you see yourself and who you are impacts how you present yourself and how other individuals respond to you. Decide who you want to be. After doing this, make sure that your thoughts, words, and actions are aligned with that identity. When you carefully plan your life and follow the steps one at a time, you win and have a successful life.

Children naturally use their imaginations and creativity as they grow up. Once they become adults, this may start to end. Many successful individuals are saying visualization is responsible for their success, and this may be encouraging for individuals who miss using the imaginations they used when they were children. Visualization is not the same for everyone, including where and when you practice it, how it is carried out, and how it affects your life. When you understand this technique and use it well, it can change your life for the better.

Visualization involves picturing in your mind the things that you desire in your life. During visualization, you think about what your life would be like if you accomplished your goals and then focus on achieving them.

Visualization is often paired with mindfulness and meditation. There are various ways in which you can visualize. It can involve finding a quiet place and visualizing.

For instance, if there is something you want to achieve, close your eyes and see yourself achieving that. If it is an award you want to be given for contributions in your workplace, close your eyes and see yourself winning that award. Think about how you will feel when your name is mentioned as the winner. Picture how you would look and what clothes you would be putting on, and even see the details about the person presenting you with the award. Imagine what the person is saying as they present the award to you, and imagine the feeling of holding the award.

Practicing visualization in your life will help you greatly. Get a quiet place where you can sit and visualize, and make sure that you will not face distractions in this place. Close your eyes and then take deep breaths to relax your body. Start to think about the situation or outcome that you want to see in your life. Think very clearly about the situation or outcome and be as detailed as possible. In addition to imagining the details, you also need to feel the emotions as you visualize.

You can do this once or more times a day, but more is better. Five or ten minutes every day is okay to visualize; you don't have to visualize for hours. When your visualization is complete, holding on to that vision all through the day will be helpful.

Understand that you can win arguments, business deals, and anything you want if you can take your time to use the right tools, which include visualization. Don't just give up because you don't want to argue or try to convince the other party at all. Arguments are an important part of life and you need to learn the right way to engage with people. An argument can be described as one or more reasons given to persuade other individuals that an idea or action is either right or wrong. It involves an exchange of opposite views. It can also bring different ideologies together to create a bond between different opposing views.

Arguments are an inevitable part of life, whether you like it or not. They can happen at work or at home. Some arguments are often useless and caused by ego. Avoiding an argument completely is the best way to win the argument. However, some individuals can consider you a weakling who cannot stand up for what you believe in if they notice that you always avoid every argument. I'm sure you don't want people to consider you a weakling. So, you need to choose your battles wisely. It is important that you know when to argue and when not to argue. If you find it difficult to stay away from an argument or confrontation, ensure that you can win the argument without attacking the individual personally or losing your cool. Heated or unresolved arguments can lead to fights. When diplomacy doesn't work and one individual loses his cool during an argument or debate, it will definitely lead to a battle. Egos are leading, emotions are high, and nobody is conceding on the present arguments. Arguments that are left unresolved can destroy good friendships, relationships, and connections to other individuals. Although it can be difficult for one to control their emotions during an argument, arguments don't have to result in quarrels or fights. Fights won't resolve the issue. You can win an argument without losing your cool or even raising your voice.

CHAPTER THREE
Winners Are Made

Winners are not born but made. This means that you can still improve yourself and become successful even if you don't have any talent or skills that you were born with.

Being a winner means pushing yourself to keep moving ahead. You don't have to be an athlete to be a winner or champion. If you have always wanted to be an athlete, but think you are not born with athletic skills, this is not the end. You may not consider yourself a natural athlete or someone who enjoys sports or exercise, but if you are determined to challenge the not-so-athletic side of you, you will see some changes. Training hard within a few years can make you the athlete you have always wanted to be. You don't know how much strength you have within you until you go out of your way to do something that challenges you and pushes you out of your comfort zone.

When you constantly challenge yourself, it keeps you on your toes and makes you see that you can accomplish any goal that you have set for yourself. When people say you can't do something, it should motivate you to prove them wrong. You need to have the attitude of a winner.

Being a winner doesn't mean that you are good at everything you do. Instead, being a winner means having the mindset of a winner in all that you do. It involves training yourself. Starting early in life to train yourself helps. Although things don't always come easy in the real world, you are prepared for it. You also become a sharp thinker and know what the next step should be.

The lessons you learn early in life will still help you in your adult life. They guide you throughout your life. Being two steps ahead can help you strategize better. It is important that you completely understand your audience and the way they engage. This is important when it comes to having an effective strategy.

A true winner never gives up. You may not win the first time you try something; however, a true winner keeps trying until he wins.

You may be upset about not winning first place for a project that you did, but you need to understand that the person who won it actually wanted it more at that time. Maybe you didn't put in as much effort and work as the winner did even though you may have done your best at that time. When you feel like you have lost, you need to remember that it was a learning opportunity for you, so you didn't really lose. You only need to keep trying, so you can perform better the next time another opportunity shows up. At that time, with your heart set on winning, you will give it your all and eventually win.

If you are not sure of something you want to do or if you are afraid of doing that thing, it doesn't mean that it is wrong. You can go ahead and try it despite the fear that the gain you will make will be worth it in the end. Be the winner you know you are. Staying committed to your goal and putting in the required effort and time makes you ready for whatever challenges you may face along the way.

You may have heard people say that winners are made and not born. So, what exactly is required to become a winner or a champion, whether in your personal life, in business, or in sports? You need to have the right mindset to become a winner. No individual is born a winner. You have to earn your status as a winner. It is not just given to you. Winning is achievable and involves repeating the same thing continuously, day after day, month after month, and year after year.

A winner's mindset is the right mentality to have. Every winner is confident in themselves and the members of their team are aware of this. The winner is never afraid to handle any challenge that comes their way no matter how big it may be. Winners believe that they are the best, and if you don't agree with that, they do their best to prove you wrong. These individuals have the mindset of champions and they believe in their skills and have trust in themselves.

You need to believe in yourself and be confident in everything you do in life. Just like athletes prepare physically, they also prepare mentally. The same thing applies to life; physical and mental preparations are needed to achieve success. Physical strength alone cannot take you far in life; you also need to be mentally strong. Although it is important to be in your best shape, all it does is keep you in the game. To succeed and become a champion, it is also important to be mentally prepared for the inevitable. Winners need to have the ability to endure criticism and they must also be able to stand up to correct what they believe is not right, especially when human rights or any kind of inequality is concerned.

When you turn on the television or go online to see high-achievers making the world better, winning Nobel prizes, breaking world records, or earning billions, one can easily assume that only the super-talented can achieve super-success.

But when you spend time digging deeper and studying the story behind winners, you will discover that they have spent countless hours or years working hard and going through a struggle, heartache, pain, defeat, and failure.

You can still achieve success even without natural-born talent. You can earn greatness through perseverance and a philosophy of strong work ethic. If you don't stop sticking to these principles, you will achieve success.

Almost any individual would like to make winning a habit. This practice is required and desired and helps individuals to stay ahead in this world that is competitive. Winning can be hard to achieve; it does not come easily. You need to consistently make dedicated efforts to win. It is attainable with dedicated and honest efforts. Since winners are made, you must do your best to succeed through perseverance and dedication.

An individual should have an inner desire to win before he even makes an effort to achieve what he wants to achieve. This is important because, winners are made from a vision, a dream, and a desire that they have deep inside of them.

Winning is important in an individual's life as it makes them aware of their hidden talents that are still untapped and their maximum potential. There are many individuals who only get to know about their true potential when they achieve success. Therefore, it is important that you make an effort to become successful.

Winning comes with accolades and many more successes thus, an individual should understand that it is important. If you are trying to achieve a goal that seems unachievable, taking the first step towards achieving that goal is important. Not all individuals achieve success as they may not have the character traits which help them to achieve success even when they are experiencing challenges. The individual has to have the desire to achieve success before they can actually achieve it. This urge is necessary as a person cannot win without it. He or she has to embrace their failures to win. You remain ahead in the race for success when you follow your ambitions and don't allow yourself to get distracted from the goals you set out to achieve.

Learning from the mistakes you have made in the past and not giving up are important when winning is involved. Winners never consider quitting as an option. They remain persistent until they achieve their desired goals. Quitters never win at all. They have no place in the midst of successful people. Every time an individual loses, they gain valuable information about how to win the next time they try. So, when they find themselves in the same position, winning becomes easier. This shows that losing a competition or battle is an important step when winning is concerned. Defeat draws your attention to your shortcomings, and this helps to get you ready for your win. Adapting a doer's attitude and remaining positive is what a person is required to do so that they get the chance to explore different options. Some individuals want something to happen, some individuals wish it would happen, and others just go out and make it happen.

Winners are made through hard work and relentless efforts to succeed. Great leaders are made through their passion for success and their hard work. You succeed even if you have failed over and over again in your life. The struggle you go through to achieve a life goal that you have been working on is the price that you pay to achieve success and this means that you are fully devoted to your goal. A winner doesn't leave the competition halfway when they fear defeat. Therefore, you must continue following your visions, dreams, and goals in any circumstance you find yourself.

You may want your child to be like a top athlete who is fearless, committed, and tough. However, when you look at the young athlete that you are raising and developing, you don't see any of these qualities. You don't see the fearless competitor. You see laziness, fear, weakness, or embarrassment, and it may be difficult for you to envision your children ever having what the top athlete has.

You are probably picturing the top athletes when they were little winning games, dominating the league, and playing fearlessly as the other children begged for mercy. But that may not be what happened in reality. In reality, the top athlete may have played the whole summer and scored zero points. They may not have any lucky shot or even a free throw, and they may have thought to themselves that they played terribly. They may have also felt embarrassed by their performance and cried about it.

Many individuals raising young athletes can relate to this image of the top athlete. Many children have this experience as they grow up in sports. They experience doubt and disappointment. Knowing this is critical to helping your children reach their potential. You need to understand that champions are built. Many individuals construct an unhealthy narrative in their minds where they are fooled into believing that some individuals were born with the mindset of a champion, and their children just weren't one of them. These individuals fail to understand that even the top athletes they look up to today experienced times as a child when they failed. This shows that your children are not backward; they are only being children and you don't expect them to have everything figured out yet. You didn't have it all figured out when you were a child too.

The top athlete's winning mentality wasn't built in a day, and neither will that of your child. Every winner goes through a process of struggling, failing, learning, improving, and then becoming successful both mentally and physically. If you are genuinely interested in helping your children reach their potential, then you need to accept the reality of what reaching your full potential takes. You have to recognize that your children don't have to remain who they are today, and you also have to understand the important role you play in their development process.

You will have many reasons to be disappointed after your child's failures. Seeing your child cry can leave you feeling sad or embarrassed, but you need to continue showing your child love and helping them no matter what.

So, if your child has a scoreless summer, you need to remember that your children are not expected to have it all together yet and that it takes time to develop the mindset and attitude of an elite performer. You need to understand that the difficult stuff that your child goes through can be a catalyst for their development and growth if you recognize and use the opportunity it provides the right way. Don't forget that your encouragement and support especially in the midst of your child's struggles and failures is very important when it comes to helping your child reach their full potential.

Characteristics of Winners

Are winners moulded by their experiences or are they born winners? While there may be certain individuals who are born winners, developing the mindset of a winner or becoming a winner or champion is something that can be nurtured. Any individual who has been a parent, teacher, or coach knows that.

What characteristics of winners do you have? How do you start?

There are many options to start with, however, you have to decide what you consider most important.

Here are some characteristics that winners have:

Winners exhibit respect and integrity

Winners exhibit respect and integrity in every area of their lives. If a winner is down at halftime, they refuse to give up and even come back with full energy to win in the second half. Winners stick to being the person they say they are.

Winners have perseverance

Each of us can set lofty goals and that is the starting point. Once that is done the next step is going after your goals with relentless persistence. All champions understand this. They know how to persist longer than other individuals do.

Winners are compassionate and courageous

All winners have the courage to pursue their goals. They have no fear of failure. They are compassionate and take calculated risks.

Winners treat every member of their team with respect and show them compassion.

Winners make sacrifices

All winners are prepared to make sacrifices. It has been said that individuals who are successful do the things that other individuals don't do, and this helps them attain the level that other individuals cannot. If there is something you really want to achieve, you must be willing to sacrifice some things that you hold dear.

Winners have a strong belief in themselves

Not every individual will believe you. In fact, you are the only individual who can believe in your dream. You will discover that everything else is possible if you believe in yourself. So, even when no other person believes in you, you need to believe in yourself. You need to have an unshakable belief in yourself and your dreams no matter what challenges you experience.

The Power of Deliberate Practice

When we see a great performer, we call them talented after seeing how successful they are. Their achievements result in people calling them talented. When success is attributed to talent, the independent and dependent variables get mixed up.

The fallacy about talent comes about because people only see the end product, which is excellence itself, and they don't see the countless hours of work that the person puts into producing it. People see an individual's perfect end product and trace it back through their life, saying the individual has always been talented and thus destined for greatness. What they didn't witness was the repetition of small tasks that led to excellent performance. If they did witness this, they would not be so quick to conclude that talent alone was responsible for the individual's success. When we use talent to explain top performance, it stops us from understanding that their success was created by a repeatable process. We also fail to understand that we could also follow the process if we choose to.

In addition to covering the ordinary sequence of actions that resulted in their success, people use talent as an excuse to justify their own failing careers. If individuals who are successful all have some innate talent from birth, then individuals without talent will never achieve any success. Many people conclude that they lack talent and therefore cannot become successful. The mindset that a person's innate talent is responsible for the person's success absolves them of being responsible for their own achievement.

When you label a person as talented, it creates a barrier between you and their performance level. The most important thing to focus on is your rate of progress. If you are a motivated person who continues to study, you will soon be ahead of an individual who started earlier than you did if they are not continuously working to improve themselves.

Anybody can attain any level of performance in almost any field regardless of when and where they begin. You just need to put in the hours of work that are required to attain that level of performance.

Ensure that you don't only focus on practicing more but practicing better. Studies have shown that simply doing more of the same thing does not lead to big improvements in performance. Individuals with high-performance levels implement qualitative changes and not quantitative changes.

When you merely increase how much you do a particular thing, that is a quantitative improvement. For instance, reading a textbook for some hours per day. In contrast, making changes to the task itself by periodically quizzing yourself over the material instead of just reading is a qualitative improvement. You can change the type of work you engage in and make significant improvements in performance without changing the amount of work you do.

You must have seen the idea of quality over quantity demonstrated in our daily lives and noticed it at the highest levels of excellence. The most effective form of training is deliberate practice. It does not only apply to sports, but it also applies to activities like speaking, coding, and writing. Deliberate practice requires constant feedback, therefore it goes far beyond what people normally see as training. It involves complete immersion in the task and pushing beyond your current abilities. This is not sitting somewhere dreaming of being a programmer while watching coding YouTube videos. It is sitting alone with a textbook solving problems and being completely focused on it.

A qualitative shift in training methods is what deliberate practice represents. It requires a change in a person's discipline to focus on a task, their attitude towards practice, and the technique they use when performing the task. Although this may look like intensive labor, high performers usually enjoy practicing immensely. High performers derive great pleasure from playing a piece flawlessly after repeating it a thousand times.

Individuals engaged in deliberate practice may even find themselves in a state where they are completely lost in a task. These individuals may be under tremendous physical and mental exertion, but they would rather be doing nothing else when they are in that moment of flow. Elite performers experience this every time they practice and not only during a competition. Deliberate practice can be hard for individuals who are not used to putting in full effort but half effort. The rewards of deliberate practice, in terms of personal enjoyment and self-improvement, make one's effort to change their training worthwhile.

When people want to improve, many of them usually think in terms of quantitative changes. I just need to read ten more pages of the textbook every night, or I just need to stay for three more hours at the office before going home. They do this because quantitative changes are able to make small differences. However, qualitative changes are required to move up to a better position. An individual can program for many hours, but writing more code will not make them a CEO. Instead, they would need to make changes in the things they do every day, starting their own company, or managing people.

When you see individuals striving to move ahead by working longer hours, you need to ask yourself if you can move further by changing what you spend your time doing but not by spending more time at the office. You can do this because quantitative increases don't have greater leverage than qualitative changes.

People are of two groups in the world when it comes to how they see opportunities. They include those who make the best use of opportunities and those who find them absolutely terrifying.

Innate talent is not the only thing that makes someone successful. Some people believe that nothing can stop them from achieving success whether they have innate talent or not, while others use their lack of talent as an excuse for not being successful. Many people believe inherent ability is responsible for success. This way of thinking absolves these people of responsibility for the low productivity or low level of performance that they have.

Their mindset is fixed, and this is tempting. They believe that if they are not born with talent, then there is no need to even try to be high performers. People with a growth mindset believe that their abilities can be developed.

If all it takes to get perfect scores in school is to shift twenty minutes of time you spend watching TV to studying, read the essay one more time, get a professor to help after class if you are stuck, and show up to the recitations, why does every individual not get perfect scores? These things are easy to do, but it is not enough to just do them right once. You have to do them correctly every time you do them. Success means doing them all correctly every time you do them. When you do the right thing once, it doesn't prevent any large obstacles. However, when the right thing is done many times with no deviation, success is achieved. This is what differentiates high achievers from individuals who are not successful. The only things that matter are the little things. Each of them may appear small, but they come together to move you ahead one step at a time.

In business, effectiveness as an executive means doing certain simple things. People may talk about secrets to success, but the execution of the right practices over and over again is what success is. Also, you get to choose your level of success because these decisions are so small that you can always control them. Any individual who is capable of making the right small decision once has the ability to achieve excellence in his field. The difference between the individuals who remain at the bottom and those who actually make it to the top is consistency. The ability to repeatedly make a positive choice over and over again with no deviation is one thing that is peculiar to success.

People often look at successful people so that they can understand the secret to their success, whether it is an innate ability or a single factor that makes them successful. Then, when they find something, they give up if they don't have that innate ability or they try to emulate that trait. These approaches are not right because there is no one specific secret that results in success. Instead, doing the little things over and over again the right way is what high performance means. When you realize this, you understand that every individual is responsible for the achievement they make. There is no secret or hidden route to achieve success. When you study high performers, you will understand that innate abilities alone are not what causes top performance, small decisions result in excellence when made consistently and correctly, and significant advancements require things to be done differently.

You can easily talk about these ideas, but putting them into practice can become difficult. You may find yourself motivated to engage in deliberate coding practice now or to change your study habits, but the real test is when you have to make the change. You will find it very hard to implement the change, but you need to remember that anyone can achieve the highest levels of success. So, ensure that you stay focused on the small decisions and do your best to always get them right. Making the right choices repeatedly will help you see improvements that will lead to success. The small decisions become substantial progress and you will discover that you are responsible for the level of excellence you achieve. Discovering that you are responsible for your excellence is invigorating and also frightening.

You need to remember the following:

- You can achieve excellence by doing ordinary things right and consistently.
- You can achieve success without innate talent.

Qualitative changes in how you practice skills lead to significant improvement and not by doing more of the same thing.

Although success requires hard work, there is no inherent thing that is stopping anybody from achieving success. Success comes when one does little things in the right way and repeatedly. You don't need to perform an extraordinary task to get to the top of a field. Instead, you just need to perform small actions correctly and repeatedly to achieve high performance. It is the little things that determine success in any profession.

CHAPTER FOUR
The Mindset Of A Winner

Every story needs a winner or one that overcomes challenges and becomes great. Not every winner wears title belts or gold medals, a winner is somebody who does whatever is required to reach their goal, and does it excellently well. A winner is an individual who gets back up and goes back to work every time they fail. You just need to be the best you can be in order to win.

Winners do not allow intimidation to stop them, they have strong determination and self-belief, and they immediately stop negative thoughts by replacing them with positive self-talk. They are able to control their emotional state and thoughts under pressure. Winners love to train themselves, make improvements, and accomplish their goals.

Winners don't usually quit. They might find themselves losing sometimes, but that doesn't make them quit. They keep trying until they win. When they make a mistake, they see that they are human and then they pick themselves up and continue moving ahead, but they don't allow themselves to quit. Although it is not ok to quit, it is ok to find yourself discouraged. You might try to do something and not always win, but you need to understand that you are human and that is life. You have not really failed as long as you always learn from the mistakes you make, never allow yourself to give up, and never stop moving ahead. When winners don't win, they learn. All winners have times when they fear, but they don't allow it to prevent them from doing what they want to do. Winners don't stop trying and they do not allow the pressure of the moment to confuse them.

Winners don't lose sight of their goal. They don't waiver from the commitments they make and no one has to tell them to work before they do. They know what they have to do. They perform when it is time to perform and they work when it is time to work. Winners achieve their goals. They stop at nothing to accomplish the goals they set. In sports, victories, belts, trophies, and medals are used to measure a winner or a champion. In our daily lives, being a winner is a state of mind that provides you with the strength to accomplish your goals, stay calm under pressure, and get over adversity. A winner is so hungry to actualize their vision, that they put in so much work and don't even care how much work they have to do to get there.

Cultivating the mindset of a winner is not reserved only for great athletes, every one of us needs to cultivate the winner's mindset. This state of mind can be seen in individuals from all walks of life, who want to be the best version of themselves and accomplish their goals to become as wealthy, healthy, wise, and strong as possible. These individuals become the heroes of their own story. It is not just the natural talents or physical attributes that athletes have that determine if they become champions, it is their mindset that determines if they become champions. This mindset can be applied to your life just as champions apply the mindset. You will achieve success if you are willing to do the necessary work. Winners don't stop trying until they achieve what they want to achieve and then they set a new goal and continue trying to achieve that until they get it and move to the next one. Winners are intensely driven and they usually do whatever it takes to get to their goals because they are addicted to success. They are not content with just being good; they work hard to become the best version of themselves.

A winner always wants the gold and never decides to settle for silver in daily life. This means that they put in their best as they try to improve every single day. A winner creates greatness, despite everything that may be against them. They still find a way to make it happen. Winners or champions erase the word lose from their vocabulary. Losing is never an option, so they keep working until they win. They remain calm in the midst of challenges because they are prepared and ready. Other individuals might find it hard to understand the mindset of the winner and how driven they are, but these people don't have to understand. Winners usually win for themselves and no one else. They don't win because someone else wants them to. The mindset of the winner is about achieving what one used to think was impossible to achieve, and every individual can get that mindset. Everything appears impossible until someone does it.

Winners maintain their work ethic and enthusiasm for years, even when they are going through adversities. They are aware of how to deal with adversity, they remain optimistic and focused even when facing challenges. Winners are persistent and resilient, and they demonstrate perseverance when faced with an obstacle to overcome. They don't allow discouragement to affect their efforts, they just come up with new strategies to continue moving ahead to accomplish their goals. Winners don't succumb to their failures, but they make changes to their approach and continue working on achieving their goals.

Winners are relentless in their pursuit to achieve their dreams, and they consider nothing good enough except the best version of themselves. No matter what happens, they prefer being the very best version of themselves. When there is a problem to be solved, they don't leave others to carry it alone and hope things get resolved, they do all that is possible to resolve the issue and make things work. They raise their standards and put themselves in a position to achieve success. Being a winner or a champion means that the individual is never truly satisfied with where they are. They are happy when they accomplish their goal but as soon as that goal is complete, they move on to work on the next goal. They dedicate their energy and time to achieving their dreams and goals. They are courageous and willing to take risks to reach their full potential.

Being good means that you do well, and it is better than being average, so nothing is wrong with being good. You perform your job and do well at it. Good means that you accomplish goals that you are proud of and you work hard. However, when winners or champions are involved, being good is not enough. Good doesn't mean you are the best version of yourself and it doesn't make you a winner. Winners have a different level of work ethic. They are proud of the work they have done, but they are never content enough to remain in that position. They keep pushing higher and harder. They strive to perform well all of the time, and not just some of the time. And they do this repeatedly, even on days that they don't feel their best.

Being a winner is not about luck, connections, wealth, resources, or talent, it is about work ethic and resourcefulness, doing whatever is required to attain your goal. Winners don't boast about their talent to get results, they get results by spending hours improving their skills and working on their craft. Natural talent is important, but skill is also important as it is earned by being responsible for yourself and doing the required work. Being a true winner or champion has little to do with talent. There are many individuals who are physically gifted and naturally talented, but they don't always achieve success. Winners don't achieve their potential by doing the minimum amount of work required to win and then boasting about their talent. They take control of their lives and do their best to reach their goal. Becoming a champion is not about genetics, it has nothing to do with what you are given or what you are born with. Champions are differentiated by their mindset.

Their confidence is based on actual evidence and not on delusion. When they become successful, they enjoy the moment and celebrate briefly, then they continue working because they still have more work to do. Winners see every achievement they make as a stepping stone toward the goal they need to achieve after that. As soon as they accomplish one goal, they start making plans for the next goal. Winners crave the end result intensely and are addicted to the thrill of succeeding.

Winners are convinced that they will win. They believe in themselves. Not every individual who believes that they will win actually wins because if a person doesn't think that they can win, then they don't have any chance of winning at all. When a person is convinced that they are going to win, winning then becomes a possibility, but that option of winning is taken off the table if they don't believe they can win. When a person is more committed to physical and mental training than their opponents, then winning becomes an option. Winners don't just complete a job, reinvent it, excel at it, define it, and even exceed expectations. They own their work, they own their potential, and they own their craft. The single mother who works two jobs to make sure her children have food to eat and the bills are paid, does whatever is necessary to do the job. She is a winner.

Winners also perform their job behind the scenes, without the glitz and the glamour, and without applauding fans. They work to be successful and not for the attention it will bring them. No individual has to see them doing the work, they just get the job done. A winner does more than anybody could ever expect of them, even when they are being watched by no one and not being applauded or congratulated by anyone. True winners don't care about the bling, but the results of their work.

Winners honor their commitments. A winner is trustworthy and has integrity. They are aware that trust can be quickly destroyed. They don't blame other individuals when things don't go right. Instead, they take responsibility and ask themselves questions about what they could have done differently to make the situation better. Winners don't cheat, but they bend the rules when necessary. When everyone else is panicking because everything seems to be going wrong, they are observant and calm, their determination is unwavering, and their composure is unshakeable.

Winners are defined by their commitment and effort and not by the successes they achieve, even though they are closely connected. Losers might be talented, but they don't make any effort and lack the drive to do any work. For this reason, they don't become successful. They compete to take part in the competition, not to win. They don't have what is required to be a leader, so they are usually followers. These individuals might be good, but they don't put in enough to become great. They don't give their best even though they work hard. They simply perform the minimum amount of work that is required. As a result of this, they never achieve greatness. Although these individuals might achieve some level of success, they won't achieve as much as they are capable of if they commit. They lack a compelling vision and they also have no powerful enough reason to create their vision. The individual who wastes his potential is a frequent story in life. The unfortunate thing about this is that they have the capability of achieving so much more.

Winners win and find high levels of success. They study the competition and prepare ahead of time. They plan the right strategies to use for their opponents and train hard to win. Winners get results, so people look up to them. They operate on an entirely different level. They perform well because they practice until they get it right and can't get it wrong.

Competitors are different from winners and losers. Competitors make an effort to put in the work and make decent progress, while losers don't even bother to put in effort at all. They avoid pressure and hard work at all costs. Competitors look for the path of least resistance and do their work. They avoid pressure, but winners don't mind the pressure. Although pressure may make winners highly uncomfortable, they still perform under pressure. Winners have the feeling of success when they perform their jobs; they don't need the attention and approval of other individuals to feel successful.

A loser usually eats whatever they feel like eating and a competitor chooses their food but cheats sometimes. A winner pays special attention to their nutrition as they pay to their training. If a competitor is given the opportunity, they might win the game, a winner creates the opportunity and uses the opportunity. A winner doesn't need a pep talk to stay motivated; they don't lose motivation even though other individuals will need a pep talk to stay motivated. When everybody else is tired and decides to give up, winners push themselves harder and keep going. They keep pressing on. When everybody else panics and they don't know what to do, they look to the winner or champion for advice and help.

These observations certainly ring true a great deal of the time and provide you with more insight into how winners think. You can develop the traits, habits, and beliefs of a winner and apply them to your everyday life. You can do this by consciously striving to develop these traits, habits, and beliefs with determination and hard work. This mindset can be applied to your life the same way champions do to their sport. Learning how the most successful individuals in the world think, fail, learn, and succeed, and what makes them champions will help you a great deal. It will help you to level up your game.

While most individuals are not professional athletes, it is possible to develop the mindset of a champion. We can attain peak performance by remaining professional when going through challenges and approaching the challenges like a champion. Every individual has the ability to discover how powerful they are inside and unleash the champion that is within them. By now, you should already be motivated to make improvements to your life, but you need to increase your productivity and take serious action to achieve results. You already have everything that you need to become great within you. Every one of us has something great inside that can make us the hero of our own story. You may lack the ability to play basketball, football, jump, run, or fight like the greatest athletes in the world, but you can learn from these people's strategies, habits, goals, relentless drive, and work ethic to develop your own champion mindset. Ask yourself what you can do to act and think like a champion today and reach your goals faster.

You must be eager to learn and always remain a good student. Having the mindset of a champion means putting in a gold medal effort, wherever you find yourself, whether you are in the competitive arena, in the gym, at school, or at work. Will you be able to sacrifice what is comfortable in the moment and what you want in the short term in order to achieve your goals? What goal do you have? Will you stay committed to doing whatever it takes to achieve your goal? How do you see the best version of yourself in your mind? Describe this person as much as possible. Write down a detailed description of this best version of yourself and becoming this person should be all you think about when you train every day.

Are you always running late or arriving early for training? Are you preparing ahead for your training, or not? Are you going the extra mile to achieve success? Behave like a winner and take the path less traveled, or stay in your comfort zone and follow the path of least resistance. Remember that it is important to take advantage of the opportunities that come with each day, and be the best that you can be. Excellence should not be scheduled for the future; it should be achieved today. Now is the right time to begin working towards achieving success and becoming a winner. What plans do you have for today? What mini goals are you set to achieve today? Are you taking steps toward your major goal? You need to win today, whether it means giving your best effort at work or school, crushing your workout, paying attention to your nutrition, or remaining mindful during skill training.

The first thing to ask yourself in the morning when you wake up is "What can I do to be a winner today?" You must be ready to do what other individuals won't do so that you can achieve what others can't achieve.

Developing a Winner's Mindset

What does developing the winner's mindset take? We will take a look at some steps to take to develop a winner's mindset. The winner's mindset is a fascinating thing to study.

We may wonder what makes some individuals stay motivated and focused on their goals. What makes some individuals succeed where others would not succeed?

These questions are quite intriguing, especially for individuals who are working towards accomplishing their own goals and following in the footsteps of winners.

Before you can become a winner, you need to understand who a winner is. Individuals who win come from different walks of life. These winners vary in background, industry, and age, and yet their mindset is one trait that they all have in common. A winner is a person who makes things happen, and one who intelligently executes his plans to achieve a desired goal.

But you need to understand that individuals who can truly be called winners don't just succeed one time or get lucky. Rather, winning becomes a habit as a result of their mental framework. You need to understand the main characteristics behind the mindset of a winner and how these characteristics can be beneficial to you.

If you feel you are not yet a winner, you don't have to get discouraged. You first need to adopt the right mindset to become a winner.

These steps will help you develop a winner's mindset:

- **Have a full understanding of what you want**

Fully understanding what you want to achieve in life and having self-awareness is very important. After all, you can't win when you have no idea about what you want to win. You may be watching successful individuals do unbelievable things and even wonder if you will ever achieve what they have achieved.

When you are sure of what you want to achieve, you use the world as your library to help you improve your skills and become better at your craft.

An integral part of the mentality of a winner is clarity about their goal. Knowing what you are looking for makes it easier to find it. You can't find something you don't know that you are looking for. Knowing what you want makes you sensitive to opportunities coming up around you that can be helpful in accomplishing your goal. It immediately puts you ahead, because you are able to start building yourself up to the point where you are able to achieve your goal. This may seem like luck to other individuals. But it is all a part of the plan and not luck.

- **Stay focused and remain in your lane**

When you are running a race, you can't turn sideways and continue watching your fellow competitors. It will slow you down and cause you to lose your focus. You might even find yourself crossing over to another person's lane instead of your own lane. You need to look ahead and not to the side. That is one trait of winners that distinguishes them from other individuals. They remain in their lane.

Individuals who are truly winning in life are not bothered about what other individuals are doing. They have no time for distractions because they have their eyes on the prize.

Also, winners are producers, not consumers. While the inspiration and advice of other individuals can be beneficial to them, most of their time is spent planning and also implementing their plans. So, developing a winner's mindset requires that you stay focused and avoid comparing yourself to other individuals. Just be yourself and do your thing well.

- **Accept responsibility**

You need to stop blaming other individuals for anything that is not going well in your life if you want to be a winner. Winners accept responsibility for the things happening in their lives. They take responsibility for their successes and failures as well.

This is what enables winners to continue winning because they are able to do an honest assessment of their weaknesses and strengths and do the necessary things to help them improve.

Winners do their work without thinking anyone owes them anything. They know that most individuals blame other individuals for their own failures and mistakes, thereby standing in their own way.

You are essentially absolved of responsibility when you blame other people for your problems. What this means is that you don't have to do anything to bring the problem to an end, because technically, whatever you do will not matter.

This is how individuals watch other individuals progress while they remain in the same place for years without progress.

However, because highly successful individuals take responsibility for the events that happen in their lives, these individuals are able to take steps to control their lives.

Even when your plans fail to work the way you planned them to, you benefit greatly from looking internally and studying the situation to see what you missed and what you could have done better.

When this is done, you enjoy life better as you are able to properly celebrate your achievements, knowing what you went through to overcome the obstacles that stood on your path to success.

- **Don't stop knocking on doors**

Consistency and persistence are two words that the behavior of winners has demonstrated throughout the ages. Nothing great ever comes to anyone without working for it. You need to keep working hard and saying "yes" to yourself even during the times when other individuals say "no" to you. Don't stop knocking on doors even when you keep getting doors slammed in your face. Persistency and consistency pay. You may have to experience those years and months where you don't get any great results and all you think about is how to quit. But you must remember that the journey to success can be a difficult and long one.

When you know that you are definitely in it for the long term, it makes you adaptive and creative, you accept the challenge and move ahead. Winners have no other choice but to make it.

- **Envision what could be**

You need to remember that individuals are only confined by the walls they build themselves. An important aspect of a winner's mindset is self-efficacy, which is a person's belief in their capacity to execute behaviors that are necessary to bring about a certain outcome. Avoid placing artificial limits on yourself.

If you notice that you are having doubts about what you can accomplish, you need to understand that most people's biggest mistake in life is not setting goals that are big enough. Don't forget that you need a total mindset shift if you want to achieve success. This can be scary, but it is important that you set targets that are far bigger than your goals. This is how winners think. This mindset makes it possible for them to do the things that other individuals could only dream of doing. Winners envision what could be instead of staying focused on what is.

- **Carve your own path**

Winners don't accept less. They are not comfortable being average, because average effort results in average results.

Highly successful individuals are aware that at times they might have to separate themselves from the crowd. They are aware that individuals who don't understand their vision will sometimes think they are crazy for doing the things they do. There is nothing wrong with this because a winner doesn't like to follow the crowd. Whenever you notice that you are doing what everybody else is doing, you should ask yourself why you are doing that. Are you taking the easy route? Are you scared of making the right move and being different, or do you just want to remain where you are? If being an entrepreneur is what you want, then you shouldn't settle for a job.

If becoming a volunteer and traveling the world is what you want, then you shouldn't settle for an average life.

If you are afraid of taking risks and carving out a path for yourself, even if it makes other individuals wonder and stare, you will have to live with any wrong decisions you make. So, do your best to live the kind of life that you will be proud of in the future.

Seeing things differently is where the secret of winning in life lies. If you can't think of something, you can't achieve it because you will only be able to go as far as your mind takes you. Changing your mindset will change your life. You can decide today to start thinking like a winner. Problems should be viewed as opportunities, and failure seen as something that is necessary to achieve success.

You adopt the winner's lifestyle when you adopt their mindset. Once the mental foundation is laid, you will start seeing positive results.

CHAPTER FIVE
Increasing Your Odds Of Victory

Has there ever been any area of your life that you have wanted to become more successful at or improve? Did you believe you would make the change but later failed to follow through with it? What could be the reason for this? Chances are you are allowing your mindset and circumstances to hold you back.

We have said that your mindset is very important when it comes to achieving success. Your circumstances are not as important as your mindset in this regard.

Most people have the knowledge about how to do a job, but they fail to do the job because their goals and psychology are not in sync.

Have you ever tried to set a goal that you want to achieve and failed at achieving it? How many times has it happened? I bet it has happened many times and you have even lost count.

You have tried to reach your goals but failed many times. And the many failures make you feel cursed deep down. When you look at everything and the future, they are the same. You are scared, but you don't know what to do about it. You become a little bit hopeful and then failure comes again. Then, when you try a few times and fail, you stop trying. This story is the same for many people, but you can be different.

When you are at a certain stage of your life, you will get permanently motivated by following through with a handful of goals. You may have failed at every goal you set, but if you keep trying, you will achieve success in no time. Don't allow the past to keep you from trying again; you can achieve your goals if you stay consistent. You need to break the mental barrier stopping you from trying and start moving one step at a time. As you do this, you will wake up one day and find that you have accomplished your goal. If you are the type who finds it hard to focus on your goals, you need to try harder. It is important that you focus so that you can achieve success.

No one can fix your life for you; you need to get in the driver's seat and do it yourself, and these ideas will give you the motivation to grab that victory you have been waiting for. The individuals who put in the effort and work required to achieve success usually achieve it. Yet, many individuals don't feel like they have to put in any effort or work at all. They feel entitled to success.

There are stories of overnight successes, people winning lotteries, and naturally talented singers and athletes rising to the top of their careers. People achieve these things, but some others do not achieve them. Most individuals who achieve success earn their success. They are always open to opportunities and ready to seize them. In addition to having the will to win, you need to be ready to work to win.

Your odds of victory can be increased. There is no one way that you will follow that is certain to bring you success in everything you do. There will be times when you will do what is within your power but still fail, and you don't have to stop trying. You can try many times even though you are not sure about the outcome. However, knowing the right strategies to use can increase your odds of achieving success.

You need to use the power of the unconscious mind. Your conscious mind may be limited and it is the unconscious mind that is largely in control. This is why you may save for a vacation and never travel or you may want to lose weight but still continue your old habits that make you add weight.

If you are ready to learn new things and become self-aware, you will easily achieve success. You just need to become aware of those unconscious recordings and beliefs that are controlling you. Once you identify them, changes can then be made. When you become aware of your unconscious mind, your odds of achieving success increase.

It is not that hard, right? Of course, it can be hard sometimes, and at other times, it isn't. You need to tap into the unconscious mind by asking the mind the right questions and then also be ready to listen and get an answer. In the meantime, you need to make the right decisions and take the right steps to achieve success in life.

You will find yourself experiencing times when things don't go the way you want them to go. There will also be times when things will go the way you planned. You need to be able to make the most of your circumstances and handle them in a way that increases your odds of achieving success.

Many individuals lack clarity, and this makes them take longer to accomplish their goals. You will find it easy to set goals if you know what you want. However, many people do not set goals for a number of reasons.

The reasons include:

- They have no idea what they want to accomplish. They find it hard to differentiate between a dream, fantasy, or wish.
- They lack the self-discipline to stay persistent and achieve their goals.
- They have no idea how to set goals.
- Not having an accountability partner.
- Fear of not succeeding.

When you have clear goals, your confidence will increase as you build competence and increase your motivation to chase your dream. Successful individuals are aware of what they want and they stay focused on getting it. The first thing to do is to decide on what you want and also ask yourself if the price is something you are willing to pay. When you are determined to get to your destination, you don't have to stay focused on the hindrances on the way.

Here are some ways an individual can perceive the dream they have:

- A dream inspired by overcoming a challenge or from an experience.
- Association inspired by a dream.
- Receiving motivation from watching people who are successful.
- God-inspired or given dream.
- A desire you have had right from childhood.
- Motivation by something such as a desire to impact people's lives.

You can ask yourself these questions to seek clarity of the dream you have:

- What do you want and what don't you want?
- What specific thing occupies your thoughts most of the time?
- What specific thing do you always talk about?
- What activities do you have the greatest sense of meaning doing?
- What do you want to be and have twenty years from now?
- What things do you want to do twenty years from now?
- You need to understand what you want to do, where you will do it, and how to do it.

Sometimes, you will not understand everything; you will only have a vision and see a glimpse of the end. As you move ahead, everything unfolds. You do not need to fully understand how you will get there. Just start moving even without seeing the full picture. The "how" will unfold as you move ahead. Do not give the storms of life the opportunity to distract you from your goal.

As long as you have clarity of your dream and are determined to continue moving ahead despite any storms on the way, eventually, you will gain clarity and achieve greater things than you ever thought you would achieve. Having clarity of dream is important and it gets you started on your journey. When you have gained clarity and are determined to achieve success, you start taking the necessary steps.

You need to do the following:

- Write your goals down.
- Identify the distractions and obstacles on your path.
- Find out the knowledge and skills you will need to accomplish your goals.
- Identify the individuals with whom you will need their help.
- Determine the amount of money you will need to achieve your dream.
- Determine how your dream will be financed.

When you assume that your future is going to be like your past, it can work in some limited situations. This is referred to as prediction reasoning. We live in a highly unpredictable world. What this means is that your thought process needs to go through a radical change to tackle the unknown as you work towards your goals.

Starting a business can be uncertain, and people who have achieved success in multiple companies that they started have mastered how to manage the unknown.

To follow these people's lead and make your future better, you need to do the following:

Have specific and realistic goals

Defining a goal is much easier than achieving it. The hard work you put in toward achieving your goal plays a very important role in your success. However, you will find it difficult to achieve goals if you don't formulate them properly. Your goals have to be specific. You can't just say that you want to be successful. Well, everyone wants to be successful, so you need to know what success means to you.

One individual may consider success to be getting home from work at 7 pm every night, while for another individual, success may mean becoming a company's CEO.

Measuring the outcome of your goals should be something you can do. You need to include a time frame for achieving your goal when you set the goal.

Stay positive and not negative. Your goal should be something you want and not something you want to avoid. Your goals should be realistic. Ensure that they match with your skills and abilities. Is your goal something that you can achieve within the time frame you set? Don't set a goal you know you cannot achieve. If your goal is a big one, you can break it down into smaller short-term goals. A person taking baby steps and moving ahead is better than one trying to take one big giant leap and not taking any step at all.

When it comes to striving to achieve your goals, you need to be flexible. Don't give up even if you face barriers that threaten to affect your progress negatively. Instead, your goals need to be modified accordingly. Consider letting go of something that is no longer important to you and then focus on important things.

Start with a small step

You may not be moving in the right direction, but you will never know which direction is right if you don't take that first step. You need to start with a small step. When you want to start working on a new venture, it is important that you ask potential clients what they think about your idea before you even start investing money into the idea.

Learn from the feedback

Pay attention to what potential clients think about your idea. This is important because their response is invaluable and you could get a new perspective from their thoughts. For instance, your idea may be to open a new restaurant, but you may discover that your potential customers don't appear enthusiastic because there are many restaurants in that area. But you can get your potential customers thrilled by offering a special package that the other restaurants are not offering.

Use what you have learned to move ahead

Take the feedback you have received and then reconstruct your path if necessary. Experiment with new ideas and change your direction to see the results. For instance, you can show your potential customers sample menus that your restaurant will have. You learn and then build, and you repeat the steps until you achieve a favorable outcome and your idea becomes successful.

This may be difficult, but when you repeat it over and over, it becomes a habit and translates to success. For example, travelers on a road trip are confident that a map and a GPS will guide them to their destination. Prediction reasoning has detailed plans and forecasts and works well when it comes to moving you along a path that is known. But when you are starting a new idea or running a small business, it is not easy.

When you go into the unknown with a new idea, product, service, or business plan, the prediction reasoning logic is of little use. This is why many individuals are usually the biggest impediment to their success. When prediction reasoning is used in unpredictable situations, it is bound to result in frustration and disappointment.

When starting a new project, you need to plan ahead. It is hard to gather the resources without first knowing what you need. Also, if you have no idea of the obstacles you may encounter, trying to optimize is difficult.

In situations such as these, the learning and building concept will guide you through the inevitable challenges that are present in the marketplace.

There has been a drastic change in the world's predictability, and our way of thinking should also measure up.

You can increase your likelihood of attaining success by taking specific actions that have made other individuals successful.

Let us discuss these actions:

Set clear goals

Setting clear goals is one crucial element of success. You need to be aware of what you want to achieve and map out a plan for how to achieve it. If you don't have goals, you can get sidetracked and not go anywhere.

Learn and improve your skills

No matter what field you are in, you need to continue learning and improving your skills. You can always improve your skills. You will be in a position to succeed when you keep up with new trends and developments.

Develop a strong work ethic

A strong work ethic can increase your chances of becoming successful. This means being consistent in your efforts, disciplined, and continuously putting in the required work necessary to achieve your goals.

Stay motivated and reduce your stress

You can have burnout when you have chronic stress, and this can cause exhaustion and reduced performance, and it can affect your success.

When your motivation is reduced, it makes it more difficult to stick to your goals and this is capable of making you feel uninterested. You need to take care of yourself by eating healthy meals and getting enough sleep as it will help to relieve some stress. But if you want to handle burnout, you need to get to the source of the problem. This might sometimes involve reassessing your goals.

If you are trying to accomplish too much and you are too fast, or if your goals are giving you too much stress, it can lead to burnout. Find ways to reduce your stress. You can do this by changing jobs, changing your plans, shifting your goals, or moving somewhere else.

Network with other successful people

Networking with other successful individuals is one great way to increase your chances of becoming successful. You have access to advice and resources that are valuable. You also build relationships with individuals who are capable of helping you to accomplish your goals.

Develop mental strength

An individual is mentally tough when they have the resilience to continue trying even when faced with challenges. Individuals with this mental strength are not afraid of challenges; instead, they consider challenges to be opportunities. They are confident that they will succeed, they take control of their own destiny and are committed to completing what they start.

Here is how you can improve your mental toughness and achieve success:

- Stay positive. You need to stop negative self-talk and believe in yourself. Also, look for different ways to encourage yourself and stay positive.
- Keep moving forward. Even when setbacks are stopping you from moving ahead or things seem impossible, you need to stay focused on strategies that you can keep moving forward. Develop your skills and see your failures or setbacks as learning opportunities.
- Be kind to yourself. Stay strong and care for yourself. Check regularly to be sure that you have everything that success requires.
- Challenge yourself. Looking for opportunities to try new things and learning more about yourself can create room for self-discovery.

Improve your willpower

Studies show that individuals with characteristics such as willpower and perseverance usually become successful. Understand that you can improve when it comes to your willpower and perseverance. You can become successful by learning to persist even when you are facing challenges. Also, delayed gratification can help you achieve success.

These strategies will help you improve your willpower:

- Distract yourself. For instance, if you are having a hard time staying away from your most loved snacks when trying to lose weight, you can distract yourself during those times of your weakness to avoid giving in to the temptation of taking those snacks.
- Continue practicing. Willpower takes effort and time to build, and you can build it. You can begin with small goals that require willpower to accomplish, such as avoiding snacks that are sugary. As you develop your ability to accomplish such small goals with your willpower, you may

discover that when working on goals that are larger, your willpower is stronger.

Develop a growth mindset

People can either be influenced by the fixed mindset or the growth mindset. These mindsets influence how individuals think about their abilities and themselves. Individuals with a fixed mindset believe that our intelligence is unchangeable and static. They don't believe that success comes from hard work but that it is simply a result of innate talents that a person possesses. They tend to easily give up when faced with a challenge and believe that talents are what individuals are either born with or without. So, they are quick to give up when they experience challenges because they believe that they don't have the inborn skills that will help them achieve success.

On the other hand, individuals with a growth mindset feel that they can learn, grow, and change by putting in the required effort. These individuals who believe that they can grow have a high likelihood of achieving success. When things become difficult, they look for new ways to move ahead and improve their skills to achieve success.

Someone who possesses a growth mindset believes that he has power over his life and can control the things happening in his life, while one who possesses a fixed mindset believes that he can't control the things happening in his life.

Ever found yourself feeling discouraged that you are not great at a particular thing? You may have found yourself constantly frustrated, feeling like you don't have control over what you are doing, and feeling depressed.

This attitude prevents you from moving high up. Adopting a growth mindset is much more constructive as it will help you improve.

Developing a growth mindset can make a transformative impact on your life. Whenever you feel depressed at the end of a fruitless day, it means you have fallen into a fixed mindset. This mindset is unproductive and a person with this mindset believes that their ability is limited or fixed. They think that you either have that special ability or you don't. You are either an inspirational leader, a great writer, or a great athlete, or you are not.

The fixed mindset believes that superstars are not made, but are simply born. They don't believe in fighting to achieve success.

It becomes harder to improve your abilities when you believe in that myth because it makes you have unhealthy emotions such as anxiety, insecurity, and jealousy. These feelings then steal energy, motivation, and focus from your improvement.

When you have a growth mindset, you can always get better by learning and putting in the work. It is encouraging and empowering to believe you can do better tomorrow.

Setbacks can be overwhelming. They are powerful when it comes to motivating you. A person with a fixed mindset sees their mistake as something bad. They allow it to affect their motivation to try and it keeps them from taking risks. When you have a growth mindset, you focus on the story and the process and not on some fairytale ending where you are the most talented individual. Your goal is to improve and not to focus on an external measure or status.

Obstacles on the way are a part of your journey to achieving success. So, you need to understand that mistakes and failures make you better equipped and informed to perform better next time.

The growth mindset makes you more resilient and stronger even when the situation gets tough.

If you possess a fixed mindset, it's crucial to transition to a growth mindset for personal growth and success. Although changing how you think about failure may not happen quickly, you shouldn't stop practicing.

Whenever you find yourself getting discouraged as a result of your fixed mindset, ensure that you tell yourself that making mistakes is okay. See success as a process that is continuous and allow yourself to learn from both the wins you have had and setbacks as well. Instead of telling yourself that you are not good enough, look at what worked and what didn't work, and you will know the next step to take.

You need to stay focused on yourself. Instead of comparing yourself to other individuals who appear to be effortlessly successful, compare yourself to the person you were last week or even a year before. Recognizing how far you have come is important as it motivates you to keep moving forward.

When you feel tempted to call yourself a failure, just say you haven't achieved that thing yet.

When you feel discouraged that you have failed or when you experience a setback or face a challenge, you can tell yourself that you have only not achieved what you want to achieve yet. The outlook is magically transformed from disappointment into possibility and hope. When you include the word "yet," people are given a time perspective, and the idea of learning over time is created. It helps the other individual understand that you are still learning and moving forward.

You need to believe that the efforts you are making are important. Instead of thinking you have abilities that are fixed, a growth mindset makes you believe that hard work and effort can help you grow.

You need to learn some new skills. When you find yourself facing a challenge, you need to look for ways to develop the skills and knowledge that you need to get over those challenges.

Learn from your failures. Failure is not a reflection of your abilities, and individuals with growth mindsets know this. You need to see your failure as something you can learn from and then improve. If you try something and fail at it, you might want to try doing it in a different way.

Get an accountability partner

You never travel alone on the journey to success even though the road to success is a lonely one. You do not work and live in isolation. Successful organizations are made by the collective efforts of the employees and not the result of a genius CEO. Even artists or solo entrepreneurs benefit from the experiences and wisdom of the individuals around them.

Nobody becomes successful alone. There is usually a great team or individual behind every successful individual. Surround yourself with the right company. Other individuals can provide the wisdom, knowledge, feedback, perspective, and inspiration you need to stay on track.

That is why you need an accountability partner that will elevate your chances of achieving success. You must have a person to whom you are accountable for your results and actions. The individual must be someone who can help you stay honest and on track. Many different factors come into play when the success of a startup is concerned, and being able or not to secure funding from investors or donors is one of the most important factors.

Donor donation is important for startups. Understanding how to increase your chances of achieving success is important when looking for donations.

These tips will help you:

Research and know what is required

Doing your research and knowing what potential donors are looking for is important, and you need to have this information before approaching them. You need to know the organizations they supported in the past and what the donors' priorities are.

You will be able to tailor your pitch, and your chances of getting donations will increase when you take the time to learn about potential donors' philanthropic goals and their interests.

Have a clear and detailed plan

You need to have a solid plan when seeking out donations. It is important that you have a detailed plan for how the funds will be used. Donors are interested in knowing how you will use their donations effectively and they want to be sure that a meaningful impact will be made.

Ensure that you have a clear plan for how the funds received will be used. This will make donors see how serious you are about your startup and it shows them that you will use their investment well.

Tell a powerful story

When it comes to securing funding, the story of your startup is very powerful. Donors need to be sure that the money they are donating is going to be used for a worthy cause, so make sure that you let them know why they should invest in your startup.

What problem is your startup solving? How will you make a difference? By answering these questions accurately, you can craft a compelling story that will attract donors' support.

Connect personally

Donors have a high likelihood of supporting organizations that they have a personal connection to. Ensure that you let potential donors know your startup aligns with their values and interests when reaching out to them.

If you can successfully connect personally with a donor, you will have a higher likelihood of receiving their support than if you don't make a personal connection.

Your pitch should be short

Don't do a pitch that is too long when pitching to potential donors; your pitch should be short and sweet. Don't bombard the donors with information. They are only interested in knowing the basics, so less is more. Ensure that your pitch is clear and to the point. Show the donors why your startup is worth investing in. If this is done, your chances of securing funding from donors will increase.

CHAPTER SIX
Winning An Argument

You can use the illusion of knowledge to convince individuals that they are wrong about something.

When people are asked what the reasons for their views are, they still stay confident of their positions just as they were before their reasons were given. We usually argue with others this way. Reasons are given from both sides, but nobody is considering they might be wrong or even listening to what the other individual is saying. Asking people to explain the reasons why they held certain views can help to soften stances and change minds.

You can use this technique to soften people's stances by asking them how you are supposed to do that.

We usually find it difficult to explain the reason we think what we think. And when people ask us to explain it, we get to know that we don't have as much knowledge as we thought. At this point, our confidence level is reduced and we become more open to other people's views.

If you are trying to argue with someone and win it, you just need to ask the individual trying to convince you of their opinion or idea to give you a clear explanation about how it would work. Chances are the person has not done the required work to maintain an opinion.

You will learn something if they are able to explain how things would work and why they believe they are correct. You will soften their views if they can't explain, thereby nudging them gently toward your views. You need to understand that a person might do the same to you, so it is important that you are able to explain the reason you think what you think.

Here are some tips on how to win an argument without damaging any relationships with people:

Start in a friendly manner

We know that most arguments usually begin when an individual asks someone for something. It might be a manager asking his subordinate to perform some tasks in a particular way or a friend asking his other friends to share the same beliefs with them. Since most of the arguments that people have usually start when an individual asks another individual for something, it can be done in a friendly manner. When this is done in a really friendly manner, the other individual is disarmed from arguing or refusing to do what is requested. It will also prevent the individual from going for a defensive position. Be cordial and gracious when asking a person for a favor as this will make the other individual unable to argue, make any excuses, or be aggressive.

Respect your opponent's opinions

Not every individual will have the same beliefs and opinions. Do not look down on people who don't have the same opinions or beliefs as you. Even if you know that they are wrong, ensure that you avoid accusing them that they are wrong. No one knows everything, so if you have nothing valid or good to say, it is best to say nothing. Your disagreement should be stated in a subtle way. This way, they will listen to the points you are making.

Arguments should be based on facts

Your arguments should not only be based on your feelings alone but also on facts. Ensure that you do not use your emotions as the primary weapon in an argument even though it is important when it comes to getting your message across. Do your best to keep your emotions under control and stick to the facts.

You need to occasionally mention facts and figures to support your argument. Provide strong examples to support your point. Also, if you are able to prove your idea scientifically, it will help as they will not try to contest your arguments unless your opponent is hard-headed.

Maintain focus and self-control

When you maintain focus and self-control, it will make things go in your favor, especially if the debate or argument is getting out of control. Ensure that you do not lose your cool. You are trying to prove your point and still maintain self-control and focus. When you lose control of your temper during an argument, it can quickly lead to a war of words and a physical altercation.

Be open-minded

You need to understand that not everyone will have the same opinion. Different individuals will have opinions that are different. You should do your best to understand these attitudes. Be open-minded enough to see the situation from your opponent's point of view and understand the situation. Being open-minded can help you understand the situation more and it may even benefit you.

Acknowledge your mistakes

If an argument is going on and you discover that you are wrong, don't waste time to admit that you are wrong. Acknowledging your mistakes will not hurt you. When future arguments or conversations come up, people will take you more seriously. This is an honorable thing to do and other individuals will understand your modest gesture. They will be convinced to take your side and respect you because people like to associate with humble individuals.

Ignore unnecessary statements that are of no value

When people want you to hear them, they might raise their voices during an argument. Try to pay attention to them even if some of these people will say things that may annoy you. It is not a must to give a response to everything that they say to you. When you stay calm and don't respond to them, you show them that you won't be swayed by their shouting and you have self-control. Unnecessary arguments can lead to quarrels and fights, so do your best to ignore statements that are of no value.

Get your opponent to be in agreement with you

Getting your opponent to say yes is important, and it needs to be done as soon as possible, no matter what the statement is about or how trivial the topic is. What you are doing here is to get the other individual to think of you as the enemy. They must agree with you and move over to your side. When you do this, you give them the idea that you two are like-minded and are on the same level.

Allow your opponent to speak

When an argument is going on, ensure that you listen to what your opponent is saying. This will help you understand where to make a valid attack on your opponent's argument. As your opponent continues to talk, you will see their loopholes. So ensure that you keep quiet and listen to them. You need to get your facts right and then proceed with the argument.

You can use these tips that we have discussed to convince an individual that your ways of thinking and ideas are the best during an argument. If you are sure that you are right about what you are saying, you have to fight for it. There is no need to go down to your opponent's level if you notice that their weapons are accusations, fabrications, and deceptions. Once you broaden your understanding with these tips, they can help you win an argument and achieve success in your goals.

CHAPTER SEVEN
Unleashing The Champion In You

Are you following the same routine day after day or living your life to the fullest? Do you feel like you are not doing enough and there is something more you could be achieving? If you feel this way, you are not alone. There are many individuals who think this way, but only a few of them are aware of how to break themselves out of the cycle of mediocrity and live successful and fulfilling lives.

In a world where our attention is continually demanded, it is easy to lose sight of our potential and development. We spend a large part of our time every day juggling responsibilities and duties, which doesn't leave us much time for growth. We just need to find the secret to reaching our full potential and start developing our potential.

Do you consider yourself unable to reach your potential? You are not the only one with this thought. Many people have found themselves stuck in a rut and unable to get out of that place. They may blame their family backgrounds, work, government, or even God for their predicament. When an individual refuses to take responsibility for themselves, they will find it difficult to step into who they were created to be.

You may be asking yourself the question of whether you have what it takes to live life to the fullest.

To live life to the fullest, you need to continue working towards achieving your highest potential. This involves setting goals, pushing yourself to achieve those goals, and then continuously making improvements. It involves realizing that the power to shape your destiny is in your hands and doing what is necessary to make your destiny a reality.

If you're uncertain about reaching your full potential, follow practical steps to aid you on your journey toward growth. So, if you are ready to start unleashing your full potential, read on to gain some valuable insights.

Each individual has the potential to accomplish great things. Still, a lot of people struggle to realize their potential and even unleash their full potential. But what could be the reason for this? It's because our focus is on the daily life's hustle and bustle as our dreams and aspirations move further out of our reach. What if you could find a way to make the good things in life come to you? This is possible, and it starts by embracing the power of possibility.

You can break down the barriers keeping you from discovering your passions, unleashing your full potential, and achieving your dreams. So, it is time to embark on that life-changing journey and unleash that potential.

You will find the following helpful:

Begin with a purpose and a goal

Ensure that you always begin with a purpose and a goal. What do you want to do, be, and accomplish in your life? What is your reason or intention for that?

If your goal is not clear, you will only be living your life like a lost sheep going nowhere.

One of the most fundamental keys to achieving your potential is finding out what you want to accomplish in life. When you set a goal that you want to achieve and work towards achieving that goal, your mind receives clear instructions about what you want to accomplish.

If you want to achieve something great, you must first identify the target. You don't shoot an arrow without identifying the target. You will end up nowhere if you don't know your destination. Therefore, it is important that you identify your purpose in life. Give a deep thought to your life and think deeply about what kind of lifestyle you really desire. What things are valuable to you? Once you know those things that truly matter to you, you need to pursue them.

Put in your best effort to achieve them. No matter what you have in mind to achieve, you are forming great habits and developing your potential when you put in work consciously toward something you want.

You need to set audacious goals to be able to unleash your full potential. Studies showed that goals possess an energizing function. The higher your goal, the greater the effort you will need to put in.

Most times, individuals set goals that they are already aware they can easily achieve. It's easy to go through events in life when you don't do anything to challenge yourself. But there can be no growth if there is no challenge. On the other hand, allowing yourself to be challenged doesn't mean that you should set impossible goals. Instead, you should set goals that are realistic and goals that expand future possibilities. Studies showed that individuals who set achievable and challenging goals have ninety percent better performance.

Understand your true capabilities

You need to first understand your true capabilities if you want to realize your full potential. This is the first step you need to take. Many individuals highly underestimate their abilities and the possibilities that exist within them. This makes it impossible for them to unleash their full potential. Do your best to reflect on how you can leverage your strengths and make improvements to your weak areas. It is important that you recognize that your potential is not limited by what you have to do or what you have done. It is possible to evolve into a different version of yourself; what is required is hard work and dedication.

Understand your potential deeply by watching inspirational documentaries or reading autobiographies about individuals who have achieved success despite adversity. There are real-world examples of individuals accomplishing greatness, and they help us see that nothing is impossible.

Receiving feedback from the people you respect, such as a trusted co-worker, a close friend, or a mentor, can help you when it comes to understanding your potential. The feedback you receive can open your eyes to areas of untapped potential. To understand your potential, you have to believe and recognize that you have the ability to achieve great things.

Refuse to be held back by limiting beliefs

Beliefs are powerful; they can create and they can destroy. They create your world. You need to have a strong belief in yourself to create an extraordinary life. A strong desire to unlock your potential is what you need. You must be ready and willing to pay the needed price. This will motivate you to do what needs to be done.

When you have a strong belief in something, you will attract it into your life. To make the law of attraction work for you, you need to get rid of negative thinking. Doubt leads to more doubt, but the case is different for success, success leads to more success. Change any negative self-talk to positive self-talk and practice gratitude. Fear disappears when you are grateful, and abundance appears. Practicing gratitude brings more into your life. That is the law of attraction working.

Now think about what kind of individual you want to be. What do you desire to have most in life? What will you do to give back to society? Unlocking potential involves believing in yourself. Imagine yourself as an old man or woman looking back on your life. Are you happy about your achievements? What are your regrets? Those things you missed out on are the things you must do. You will live a fulfilled life when you achieve them.

Examining your limiting beliefs can help you unlock your true potential. What have your limiting beliefs caused you to lose in the past? What are those same limiting beliefs making you lose at the moment? What are they costing your loved ones? And also, what will those beliefs make you lose in the future? What regrets will you have some years from now if you don't stop holding on to those limiting beliefs?

If you believe that you are not wired for happiness, you can replace it with something positive such as, "I live in a natural state of happiness." Do this and you will suddenly find yourself happy.

Many individuals go through life avoiding their feelings. They just want to escape themselves. But people who are aware of how to unlock hidden potential know that it requires one to deeply examine their inner self. You can only unlock what is inside you if you know what you have inside of you.

You need to stop allowing yourself to be held back by limiting beliefs as they affect your ability to unleash your full potential. Overcoming these harmful beliefs can be difficult as they usually form early in an individual's life. However, recognizing that these toxic beliefs that the individual has are not reality but that they are distorted self-perception is important.

Limiting beliefs can range from adopting a limited worldview to believing you are not good enough. These beliefs can take many forms. Having self-defeating thoughts and surrounding yourself with the wrong individuals can affect your ability to be successful.

You need to directly confront these limiting beliefs to overcome them. A great place to begin is by identifying the beliefs and questioning whether they are actually true or false. Are the beliefs simply the result of presumptions that you or others have made, or does evidence back them? Defeating your limiting beliefs can help you live a life of purpose and confidence. And you will achieve more than you ever thought possible.

Writing the limiting beliefs that you usually have and their sources in a journal can help you greatly. Many times we have negative thoughts, but they never happen. There are rare occasions where a limiting belief comes from past adversity or failure, and you can change things by rewriting the script according to what you want to see.

The most important part is finding out what works best for you. You need to identify your most limiting beliefs and confront them if you want to unleash your full potential.

Create a detailed action plan

Setting goals doesn't guarantee that the goals will be achieved; it is only one step in the entire process. Once you know your goals, the next thing to do is to create a detailed action plan. Have you ever found yourself trying to assemble a piece of furniture when you are not clear about the directions? The same applies to goals; just make sure that you set specific and clear goals.

You can begin by writing down some precise steps that need to be completed to achieve your goals. Incorporate the specific actions you need to take to achieve your goals into your daily routine. Also, extra accountability is provided when you add them to your calendar, and you will keep your focus on the things that truly matter. You don't have to overthink the process as it serves no individual. You need to act and not continue overthinking. Taking action moves you further while overthinking wastes your time.

Celebrate the achievements you make along the way, no matter how small they may be. Achieving your goals is not about the destination but about the journey. Although accomplishing your goal is important, what is far more valuable and rewarding is the person you become. When you create a detailed action plan and you are consistent, it will work out well.

Change a fixed mindset to a growth mindset

An individual with a growth mindset has a conviction that he can develop his abilities over time. Studies show that students who possess a strong growth mindset have a significantly higher score in every subject than students who have a fixed mindset. You need to cultivate a growth mindset if you are the type with a fixed mindset. While a fixed mindset makes you worried about how people will judge you, making improvements is what the growth mindset makes you concerned about.

You need to understand that you can still improve and become skilled at something even if you are not skilled at it today. This is something that an individual with a growth mindset knows. So, to effectively embrace this growth mindset, recognizing this fact is important. Many individuals are too focused on achieving their goals that they do not consider growing along the way.

However, individuals with a growth mindset focus on the progress they make daily and they are open to learning new things. A person who lived a fuller life is not the person who stayed so focused on winning that he ignored his journey, but the individual who never stopped learning, and spent time to appreciate his experiences.

You need to consider adversity an opportunity. Rather than seeing roadblocks and challenges as signs of weaknesses, take them as a chance to grow. It is important to develop a growth mindset if you desire to unleash your potential.

Get support

You will need the support of other individuals to develop the capacity to unleash your full potential. There are individuals who have already accomplished the goals you want to accomplish, and you can learn from these people's mistakes to accelerate your progress and growth. Studies indicate that individuals who write down their goals, make detailed plans, and send progress reports to their accountability partners have a high rate of becoming successful.

It is also important to seek out the mindsets, skills, and characteristics you need to develop to accomplish your goals and unleash your inner potential. When you are trying to accomplish audacious goals that will push and stretch you, you will get to a point where you need to become an entirely different individual.

We will look like the individuals we regularly spend time with. So, it is important to be intentional about who you spend your energy and time on and to ensure that the individuals you spend time with help you become an improved version of yourself. Unfortunately, so many individuals have failed to reach their full potential because of the individuals they spend their time with. Being deliberate when it comes to associating with other individuals who will help you become the best version of yourself is important if you want to unleash your potential.

You need to embrace the power of possibility as it is the foundation for successfully unleashing your potential. Great things can be accomplished when you recognize your potential, confront those limiting beliefs you have, and develop a growth mindset. Don't allow anything to stop you from achieving excellence, no matter what that thing is.

You should not settle for a life that is less than the kind of life you are capable of living. You will find passion in playing small. Ask yourself the question, "Am I living life with my full potential?"

Life is too valuable and short to settle for mediocrity.

Focus on habits

Do you know the difference between individuals who unleash their full potential and those individuals who don't? The individuals who unleash their full potential have developed the habits that are necessary to make success part of their everyday routine. They know that greatness is achieved in the small things they do every day. This means the habits they display every day. Inspiration and motivation may get you started, but it is your habits that keep you in the long term.

Be self-confident

Unleashing your maximum potential requires that you are self-confident. You deliver a better performance when you are confident. Preparation is one great way to increase your self-confidence. You need to be prepared for any opportunity that may come your way so that you don't suddenly have a great opportunity and not be prepared for it. Preparation involves training yourself in advance for future opportunities. As you continue in your training, you will continue to become better, and your self-confidence will increase if you become an improved version of yourself.

Regardless of what field or industry you find yourself in, you need to understand that preparation is important. If you are a businessman or woman, you need to improve your skills and learn everything about the business so that you can take the business to the next level. Your confidence level will be determined by your level of preparation. Don't forget this.

Focus on small changes to achieve big improvements.

One big mistake that many individuals make is trying too fast to change too much. Lofty goals can have an adverse effect even though there is great merit in setting them. An example is physical fitness. Becoming a healthier person doesn't have to take too much effort and time. Spending thirty minutes of your time every day performing some activities can be great for your health. You can decrease your risk of diabetes and heart disease, while also enhancing your concentration and achieving weight loss. Yet, when you try to get results too fast, it can result in setbacks, injuries, and even abandoning your fitness regime. So, you need to stay focused on making smaller changes and then you can start experiencing big improvements.

As you take baby steps, you build momentum. Success is not a destination, but a journey. There is no shortcut when it comes to unleashing your potential. You don't take a pill and wake up to find that you have unleashed your potential. It doesn't work that way.

You need to grow your traits, habits, qualities, and character by taking small steps. Even if you are someone who works really hard and one who works twenty hours every day, you will not suddenly become successful overnight. Success takes time. Consistent progress will help you build your momentum. Taking small baby steps every day means you are growing your momentum. You will eventually arrive at a point where success will start coming to you. The problem that most individuals have is that they quit trying and give up as soon as they fail to get their desired results.

Your momentum needs to be maintained through consistent progress. A river is able to cut through rocks because of its persistence and not because of its power. You need to be persistent like the river because you need persistence to unleash your greatness.

Stay informed

When you are going on a road trip, you need to know your target destination and your point of origin. You also need to be able to measure your progress as you move along to be sure that you are on the right track. This same principle works in different areas of our life. We need to fully understand something before we can change it. If you want to maximize your potential, you need to know the facts.

Don't live your life anyhow, leaving it to guesswork or chance. Ensure that you stay informed. Be sure of what you want, the things you need to change or do to get what you want, and what to track when it comes to measuring your growth.

Compete with yourself

Raising your standards is something you can do to unleash the potential you possess. Comparing yourself with other individuals will not do you any good. The only person you should be competing with is yourself. All you need to do is perform better than yourself. There will be no end to the comparison if you are comparing yourself with other individuals. You will always find something that you don't have and the other person has.

It is important that you set your own benchmarks. Be proud of what you have already achieved and continue making progress. As long as you are improving yourself and moving forward each day, you will be fine. You will always find other individuals who are making progress faster than you, so that should not bother you. Everybody will not progress at the same pace. That is how life works and it is absolutely alright.

Ensure that you raise your standards and do the things you must do. This means you are improving the quality of your life. If you are not getting what you want in any area, it is because you have not improved yourself. No matter what achievements or goals you want to achieve, you will never achieve them if you fail to raise your standards and continue to cling to your older self. You will rise along with your standards if you raise them.

Use visualization

Your entire world can be visually created by you. Unleashing your full potential may appear impossible, but it is made possible by visualization. You get absolute certainty from visualization. It is important when it comes to unlocking potential.

You can visualize yourself performing in an arena filled with screaming fans, and the arena can become the particular one you wish to perform in. You can even visualize the details of the performance.

Imagine being able to achieve whatever you want and living a life with unlimited potential. Won't you love that? Everybody wants to live a fulfilling and extraordinary life. In fact, no individual wants to live a life of mediocrity. However, this is not always the reality.

Most individuals don't achieve their full potential even though they desire to live a limitless life. The fears that they have block them and they believe the people who discourage them and tell them that it is impossible to achieve what they want. They allow their failures and mistakes to affect them. Life is only lived once, so living your life with your full potential is important.

What if self-doubt won't allow you to do what you have to do even though you have the potential to be highly successful? Don't you think you will regret it in the future?

No individual likes to have a life full of regrets, and nobody wants to go through life with limited potential. Now is the right time for you to get in the driver's seat of your life and start working towards achieving your full potential.

Stay committed to continuous improvement

If you are not willing to learn, you cannot improve and become better. And no individual can help you if you are the type of person who is not willing to learn. Nobody can stop you if you make up your mind to learn. The crucial factor is to stay dedicated to continuous improvement. You have to keep striving to improve and perform better than the previous day.

When you don't get what you want in life, you need to understand that someone else is not responsible for that but you. When you improve yourself and become worthy of the success you seek, you will see that success will automatically come to you. You attract what you are and not what you want.

When you improve your skills and increase your knowledge, you will attract more success to yourself. Therefore, stay focused on improving yourself. When you are committed to consistently working toward your personal growth, you will achieve success in no time.

Work with a coach

Coaching is powerful. It helps people achieve their potential. Your mentors and coaches can help you focus on the important things, follow through on the commitments you have made, and develop the habits that will help you achieve success. Everybody needs a coach to become better versions of themselves and reach their maximum capabilities.

These principles can help you achieve great things in life.

Personal Development and Self-care

Every individual seeks to become the best version of themselves and to reach this level, one needs to reflect on their lives. Alongside assessing your strengths and weaknesses and honing your skills, prioritizing self-care is essential to unlock your full potential.

If you want to develop yourself, you need to start with self-care. You need to pay attention to self-care and improve your physical and mental health, improve the quality of your relationships, and reduce your level of anxiety and stress to reach your full potential.

Personal development involves all the activities that you need to engage in to improve every area of your life such as activities that will increase your wealth, talent, and potential. Your professional and personal life also improves.

Personal development and self-care go hand in hand, and you need to know this if you wish to work on yourself. You can't develop yourself without self-care.

Here is what to do:

Do a personal assessment of your life

Think about the areas of your life that need improvement. Maybe it is the way you handle conflict, the way you manage time, or your commitment to a goal you set. When you assess yourself, it helps you know your shortcomings so that you can improve them.

Practice meditation

Meditation helps you to silence the noise in your mind. You are able to slow down and relax. You don't meditate to just stop thinking about anything completely, you meditate to observe your thoughts and reflect on how your life is affected by the thoughts. Daily meditation will give you a clearer state of mind, even if you meditate for five minutes.

Be serious about time management

Many individuals have problems with time management. You may have noticed that a lot of time has passed and you haven't done anything productive or useful. Instead of spending too much time endlessly scrolling through social media, you can simply read or watch educational or inspiring videos about your topic of interest.

Give yourself credit

You need to acknowledge your achievements even if they are not big. Give yourself a reward after every success you achieve. This approach will serve as motivation to achieve additional goals. Your confidence in yourself and your abilities will also increase.

Don't stop learning

When you learn something new, it is motivation on its own. You will discover more new interests as you learn new and different things.

Push yourself to go further

One good way to motivate yourself to push past your limits is by challenging yourself. No matter how small the challenges you overcome may be, you will have a push forward, and your determination to go further and achieve more will increase.

Make your health a priority

You won't be able to achieve personal growth if you are not in good health, emotionally and physically. Maintain a healthy lifestyle and diet, and don't fail to get enough exercise and sleep.

Many individuals want to learn how to unlock their potential. You need to understand that your brain has the capacity to do whatever it chooses to do. The human mind is a source of immeasurable power and energy. This has been proven many times.

There are stories of individuals who suffered a stroke and suddenly knew how to play the piano, and who had an accident and suddenly started speaking another language after they woke up. This is known as acquired savant syndrome. It proves how incredible the human brain is, and it has been documented in only a small number of people worldwide.

In our daily lives, certain functions may be actively suppressed by our brains in order to help us stay focused on our primary needs. Unfortunately, being a world-class athlete and a brilliant mathematician are not basic survival needs. But we always have the capacity to do these things.

CHAPTER EIGHT
Sustaining Winning

Winning is important in life, and when you win, you may want to continue winning. When you were a child, you may have been told that it doesn't matter if a person wins or loses, and that what matters is how the person plays the game. You may have heard that what is important is the person's level of participation. However, is this applicable to every situation in our lives? I don't think it is. When we say what is important is the person's level of participation, are we not also saying that losing is acceptable? For this reason, young people are encouraged to confront the views of being losers. Winning is important and you will learn from experience that simply losing or taking part in something is not important.

Winning gives an individual their identity. No individual enjoys losing. Or do you? Every human desires victory; it is in our nature. Participating in an event might make you have positive feelings, but it is winning that actually matters. When you have experience in participating, losing, and winning, you will see that winning is everything. You need to believe in yourself and fight for what you want.

Humans have a collective memory of past events that makes them do some of the things they do. They make us have a certain kind of feeling about something. Many years ago, people on Earth lived in small hunting groups, and the only options they had were to either find food to eat or die if they couldn't find food. Today, the human brain still sees winning and losing as important life-and-death situations. And this is what makes winning important to humans.

We leave a lasting impression on people when we win. Success continues to build until winning eventually becomes the norm. You want to leave a legacy that you can be proud of because you made the best use of your opportunities and abilities.

Simply participating will not make you become successful, and this is the reality in almost every area of life including sports, careers, academics, and personal relationships. While past generations could succeed when they just participated, today's reality makes us believe that winning is everything.

Winning in life means you are achieving your goals and living your dream life.

How to Keep on Winning

We live in a society that is thirsty for "winning." People want to reach a professional level status in their given profession or sport and be praised by millions of fans as Demi-Gods. As we keep winning, we keep appearing more successful, but what is our definition of winning?

What path should we take to win? Psychology in sports is powerful, and this is undeniable. Each athlete undertakes this internal process at their own pace and in their own way. Your frame of mind is the most important thing in your failure or success and building your mental toughness begins with setting goals.

What result are you searching for? What achievement do you want to make today or even in some years' time? Successful individuals already know where they want to end up even before they start moving. The attainable and clear goals that they set propel them to their success, no matter what those goals may be.

First, you need to check the ego at the door, as it is capable of limiting you. What may drive and fuel a person's ego sometimes is the pressure to win and the pressure of society. So, you would find it beneficial to focus more on your tasks. Having the drive to win is okay, but if you are an athlete and planning on competing for a while, you would find it more beneficial to focus on how you play. You may have heard or seen quotes from different successful athletes about how they did everything they could and felt good even when they lost. Many dedicated athletes have credited their team for their achievements and put in their very best knowing they cannot control the competition's outcome. The only thing they can control is their effort and their focus. So, they stay present in the game and focus.

Let us begin by setting a goal of shifting your thoughts from trying to control what you cannot control to what you can actually control. You can focus on the work you put into improving your skills. Doing the necessary work and perfecting your skills may also help to motivate the members of your team to do the same and make you the team leader. This fuels the ego as it becomes a win-win. Greatness is quite infectious and, because few individuals are leaders and most individuals are followers, you are creating a positive environment by keeping your team motivated to perfect their skills. This will lead to good things. So, what is winning to you? Is it the instant satisfaction of winning the competition or game that is the most important to you? Or is it knowing that you are on the right track and growing as an athlete and you will succeed another day, should you lose the competition or game?

You will not always win every fight or game, and this is the reality of life. When you set small goals, you work on them and improve as you continue working because you know that you will perform better the next time there is another opportunity.

Winning After You Lose

Losing hurts, and everybody wants to win even after they lose. Nobody enjoys losing. Anybody who says otherwise is not being honest with that. Yet, even when you lose, you can still win. A minor mindset shift is required when a person is learning how to win when they lose. You will notice that it becomes easier as you continue to practice.

The following are ways to do that:

Focus on your strengths when you lose.

You won't find losing pleasant, even if you are in the best of times. During your worst times, losing can make you feel like the whole world is against you. Don't allow yourself to succumb to that self-defeating way of thinking. Instead, you need to make a list of the strengths you have and then use them. Some of these strengths that you possess have not been used for a long time. You need to learn to start using your strengths. They will help you challenge yourself to try again and win.

Competition makes the world lively

If every individual in the world had an equal amount of ability and talent, the world we live in would be quite boring. Competition makes it lively and not boring. When you see what other individuals are doing, it makes you stay engaged, increases your determination, improves your skills, and increases your motivation.

Are you doing whatever you are doing to win? Do you want to achieve success? Keep your eyes on yourself even while paying attention to what your competition is doing, and you will definitely win again. In this instance, you also win after you lose.

Losing can push you to renew your commitment.

How badly do you want to become successful at the endeavor you failed? You can renew your commitment to the goal when you have the right mindset and desire a successful outcome. Developing a winning strategy will be beneficial to you in life.

Giving up is not an option

This is probably not the first time that you have participated in an event and lost. You also don't have it within you to give up. Remember those challenges you tried so hard to overcome and continued to work despite how difficult it was? Those losses were big ones, but you stayed steadfast and didn't give up. This can-do attitude will help you win again. Continue with it and you will find yourself at the finish line soon.

See the broader picture

You may find it difficult to see past the recent loss you have experienced. Yet, you need to do exactly that after you lose. If you cannot see the broader picture, you will never have the motivation to keep moving. Your world is not a box that you can't escape. It is waiting for you to discover it. Knowing this should motivate and inspire you to continue moving ahead. You need to understand that the loss is a step toward success.

Learn from your loss

If every individual loses at one time or another, the important thing is to learn something from the experience. If you keep worrying that you have bad luck or the timing is wrong, you are not gaining anything from that. Try to figure out what you didn't do right and learn from your mistakes. When you have fully understood what made you fail, you are already a step ahead of performing better the next time the opportunity shows up. This way, you have already changed a loss into the first part of your win.

You become a person with empathy and compassion

No individual likes a winner who is arrogant. It takes a person who has lost to truly understand the feeling associated with losing. When you lose, you will know exactly how the other individual feels when they lose. This makes you an individual with empathy and compassion. Your inflated ego will be kept at bay by this compassion the next time you are in the winner's circle.

Learn from your network

You need a separate set of ears and eyes, so you will find it helpful to share the experience of the loss you recently had with your network, you might learn some things from them that can help you win the next time. Discussing all that happened and listening for techniques and suggestions that worked for other individuals is usually enough to help you win again. Listening to how other individuals got back up after they lost will also make your loss feel less painful.

Make use of what worked in the past

You have put a lot of effort into your work, but it didn't work out well as expected. Even though it didn't work out as expected, you are already invested. Therefore, there is a lot of sense in making a profit from the time and effort you have invested in this and looking for new ways to perform the task. Try to remember what worked well for you in the past and add those techniques and strategies to the task.

Be prepared for a potential loss

Before you even start thinking about how to deal with loss or failure, you need to get yourself properly prepared for the worst that may happen. Be hopeful that you will achieve the best and then be prepared for the worst. You might even experience several failures before you start taking some things seriously. When we talk about preparing for the worst when one takes a risk, we do not mean catastrophizing the potential risks, focusing on negative thoughts, or convincing yourself not to take any action at all. It involves being smart about the risks that you take and ensuring that it won't take you a long time to get out of the mess that an unexpected failure can leave.

Don't stop holding on to your dream

Our dreams keep us moving ahead during our darkest times. Those dreams that we have had for a long time are nature's way of getting us to keep moving ahead, especially when everything is not going the way we want it to. Your dream may not be achieved when you want and may take a little longer to get there, but taking small steps can help you make progress and achieve your dream. This shows that you are not a loser, but a winner. You may have experienced many failures in the past, but you must ensure that you never stop holding on to that dream, and you will definitely accomplish it.

More About Failure

We will discuss things you can do to properly prepare yourself for failure before you take the necessary action.

Smart risks protect you better from a big loss. Smart risk, stupid decisions, and big risk big reward are three potential types of risks that an individual may take.

Making a stupid decision is the first type of risk any individual can take. This is when a person takes a risk that gives them a very low chance of winning, a very short period of enjoyment, or one with a small potential reward. The risk is big, but the reward is small.

Some examples of this type of risk include playing the lottery, taking too much sugar, taking a loan to buy a house or car you can't afford, lifting weights that are too heavy just because you want to impress your friends, doing business with someone or marrying someone without knowing them well, and cheating during exams.

Big risk big reward is another type of risk, which is quite popular. A lot of people make assumptions that you must make big gains from the big risks that you take. Then you follow this belief and put all that you have into the project, and when things go wrong, you lose everything you invested. When you take big risks, there is a probability that you will lose. So, why would you allow yourself to face this when there is a big chance that you will lose?

Investing in something you don't have a full understanding of, changing your job without properly researching the company you joined, borrowing money from a lender to start a business because you think your idea is great, overtraining in the gym because you are looking for fast gains, and starting a new diet without properly doing your research and gaining knowledge about it, are examples of decisions termed "no pain, no gain."

Smart risk is the third type of risk. The downside of these risks are small and manageable and they have enormous upside potential.

When you take the smart risk and fail, you don't lose much. However, if you take it and win, your win is big. These opportunities are not common; they are very rare. To take a smart risk, you have to patiently check every opportunity until you find the right one.

Success does not only involve moving from failure to failure until you arrive at the top but also not taking every opportunity that comes your way until the right one shows up. A person who takes a smart risk is smart enough to be in a position where rewards are big and risks are manageable. Building skills that are rare and in high demand so you can easily get a job, fully understanding one type of investment than most people and waiting patiently to make a move at the right time, having some potential customers before you start your business, and hiring the trainer who is best at preparing a diet and exercise plan for you and then consistently sticking to it, are examples of smart risks.

When an individual takes a smart risk, the failure that might come can be easily managed and the person won't find themselves in a lack of resources. Risking everything you have can make you fall badly if the investment fails, and this will take you many years to get back up.

Many individuals get so emotionally stricken after a big failure to the extent that they remain in their comfort zone for a long time, or they might struggle with their finances for many years.

So, before you make the decision to take any risk, you need to answer these questions:

- Is there anything that could go right? What is it?
- Can something go wrong? What is it? Can I manage the risks, and what will I do in case of failure? Make sure you are clear about the answer to this second question when you answer it.
- How much time and money are you prepared to lose?
- Do you have options if things go wrong? What are those options?
- Do you have safety nets installed?
- What damage will failure cause to your health, relationships, and so on in case things don't go as expected?
- If you don't take the risk, how much will you regret?

Don't understand this wrongly. Many times, the biggest risk you can take is not doing anything or taking an action in your life. Being goal-oriented, proactive, and bold is important.

You don't have to be afraid to make moves towards what you want to achieve, be it changing your career, starting a relationship, starting your own business, and so on. But that doesn't mean you should not be smart when it comes to making decisions. You must not take uncalculated risks and make unwise decisions. Doing a detailed plan and calculating the risks before venturing into anything will help you a lot.

Having a learning period is a wise thing to do even if you are waiting for the opportunity that is right for you, one with the potential of a big reward and a small risk.

Sadly, the markets have become very crowded, complex, and volatile, and therefore, it is very difficult to make it big the first time. What this shows is that you can rarely succeed if you don't have a proper learning phase. Do your best to experiment with what works as well as what doesn't work. This is the consciously planned phase where you learn about yourself, the markets, and other people. It is also called the search mode.

Whether it be starting a new business, switching a career, finding their dream partner, or making decisions to pay more attention to their health, people can achieve success in as little as a month, and some can even take a decade to achieve success.

Making adjustments to your business idea to make it what customers want, understanding the rules of investing by making a few bad investments to learn about investment, experiencing some breakups to understand what you really desire in your partner, and moving from one job to another to find what work is best for you, are some of the search mode's validated learning examples.

You learn from the search mode until you are able to achieve success. This period includes small failures until you achieve success. But you consciously stay focused on validated learning because failing feels emotionally hard.

Thus, you rather learn what works for you and what doesn't work. Writing down everything you have learned, making new plans to experiment with, and making progress even if the drivers that move you through the learning phase are emotionally painful things. The point is that you can't fail in the search mode. You only learn.

What this means is that you can make plans part of the learning curve and know which things you need to understand in the search mode, but you will need to make some adjustments on the road. You need to understand that everything takes over three times more resources than expected.

Let's forget about the rewards, risks, and learning, and say that you simply failed hard. The first question people usually ask themselves is "Should I let go or persist?"

A failure is usually a very demanding position, rationally and emotionally. Managing your emotions and making your next move at the same time is important, and this can result in confusion.

For instance, you might be tired and disappointed, but you might be asking yourself whether your success is just close. Or you might be trying and still be in love with your idea even though you can't even see the light at the end of the tunnel.

A mixture of negative and positive emotions such as planning the next step to take to turn the situation around and win usually exists.

Actually, you can find out if you should let go or persist by simply assessing these two things honestly.

1. The experiments that you can still do.
2. The resources you have.

When a person fails, there is almost always a connection with losing resources. But going through the experience of failure is much more difficult if you have completely run out of resources. This makes it even harder to persist at that thing.

That is why it is important for you to at least have some safety nets as you take smart risks because if you run out of time or money, it's over.

So, you need to first assess how deep you are in the hole.

The following reasons might make you quit when you discover that you are too deep in the dip:

- You become too scared to continue because of failure.
- You run out of financial resources.
- You run out of time.
- You lose your passion and interest.

- You are no longer serious about continuing.

If you run out of time, financial, or emotional resources, you don't have many options left. Don't rely on miraculous solutions, fast turnarounds, or bringing yourself out of the hole you are stuck in overnight.

When you fail, it doesn't mean you have lost the whole war. It may mean that you have only lost a battle. So, you need to calculate how you will get back the resources you need to continue with the new plan you come up with. Putting together resources to invest them in a project that is failing is a tough place to be in.

It is faster to invest money than to earn money, and this means that you need to set limits on the investments you make and consider that you will have slow progress.

Your progress is the next assessment that is even more important. Do you completely understand what else you need to learn to make progress, or are you confused and don't know what step to take next?

Do you know when to quit? When you have everything that you can and you make no progress, that is when to quit. At this stage, you get to the maximum, but the position is not sustainable.

So ask yourself the question if a sustainable position can be built around taking more risk.

Based on the remaining resources available and your plan, make a simple calculation based on the following question. Did you make progress with your last five experiments and how many more experiments can you comfortably do with the remaining resources? You should get a clear answer that will guide you on whether to quit or persist.

If you still have ideas and resources after you failed, proceed, but do so with caution. You can fail faster, but make sure that they are small failures that don't affect you badly. Failing faster means you learn faster and your resources are properly managed. You can decide to quit if you run out of ideas and resources. This way, you can move over to something even better.

The toughest one is when you still have experiment ideas but you are out of resources. Risk takers, especially individuals who are not from wealthy families, frequently find themselves in this position.

If you are in this category, you should move on, but in a rational and smart way. You need to limit how much more investment you will put in, how long you will keep trying, and also how real progress will be measured.

You need to know that you must experience real progress by staying on the same path. Ask yourself questions that will help you know if you are making progress.

If you do a few experiments and still don't make any progress, and you find yourself running completely out of resources, there is a possibility that you will burn out soon. So, you need to slow down before it gets to that point and look for a new opportunity.

There are nice stories of individuals who persisted for many years until they became successful, but most individuals burn out in a period of three to five years. There are success stories that are exceptions.

It is important for you to be realistic and serious about how long to keep trying, and you must make sure that you manage your experiments and resources wisely. Ensure that you have a detailed plan. Make a detailed plan about what you will doing, how long you will be doing it, and when to stop and switch to something else if it doesn't seem to be working out. Also, do a detailed plan on what you will be switching to.

An emotional confusion that usually happens when failure is concerned is that you really like what you do and don't want to stop doing that beautiful thing, even if you don't seem to be making any real progress.

You want to continue doing it because you enjoy it. This can happen especially in business whereby you have a great view of your business, but you are not getting the feedback you want from the markets. Sadly, the markets always win.

In career, entrepreneurship, and business, you desire progress. You need progress that is measurable. When we talk about progress in business, it refers to money. The business needs to create value and make money, otherwise, it is just a hobby.

If one thing is not working, just look for something else that you can make money from and still enjoy. If markets are not willing to reward you for something that you really enjoy doing, it is not a business but a hobby. You can still try to do it, but you might find yourself frustrated while hoping that you will experience a change from the market.

Should you only think about the money? No, that shouldn't be the case. However, if there is something you really love doing, you can get the best-paid job for it. Should money not be on your mind at all? You should be thinking about creating value first and the money will come. You are not creating any value if you are not making money in business.

Having hobbies, which might bring no money, is completely okay. You can also have another thing that you are good at and which you love and enjoy a little bit less but give decent earnings.

Finding that thing that you do so well and get paid to do is great, but you shouldn't be so focused on thinking about that. That doesn't always happen. If surfing is what you are great at, it doesn't mean that other individuals will pay you to do that.

Failure affects emotions the most. Failing hurts everyone. It is hard to cope with, and this is something every one of us needs to admit to ourselves.

Some individuals are better than others when it comes to handling failure. Although these individuals are emotionally better equipped to handle it, it causes every one of us pain. If you believe in yourself and have strong trust in the world as well, you will find it easier when experiencing failure. Also, you will find it easier if you had the kind of upbringing where failure was not considered something bad.

But in this case, failure still affects you emotionally. When negative feelings are suppressed, they can later backfire and lead to anger, bitterness, and depression. You need to allow yourself to process the failure emotionally.

When you want to heal faster after going through failure, you can do the following:

- Ensure that you don't go back to the situation you found yourself in before taking the risk.
- Even if you feel that taking action immediately makes sense, you need to take some time off to grieve. Relax and pamper yourself.
- Constantly reassure yourself and reward yourself for your early wins.
- Use success mantras.
- Don't overrate things and see them better than they actually are.

Failure takes time to heal; this is the first important fact when dealing with failure emotionally is concerned. The individual who has experienced failure goes through different phases which include denial, anger, disappointment, depression, and acceptance.

Understand that going through failure is not a one-time event, but a process. This means that it will take you time to heal as there will definitely be ups and downs. The grief associated with failure can even take up to several months.

Taking some time to heal also requires that you should pay attention to self-care and be gentle towards yourself. Although this may sound funny to some people, it is known as self-mothering.

Failing is difficult enough. Being too hard on yourself will hurt you more, so don't keep thinking about why you let yourself fail, why you didn't play your cards well, and so on. Be understanding and also be compassionate and gentle towards yourself. This is important to make the emotional recovery process faster. The emotional side of you will instinctively want to return to the situation you were in before the failure. What happens is that you become scared, and you don't want to move on but to go back to a safe spot. And you then believe that there is no safer place than the situation before you took the risk.

But that is usually not a good move, or there would have been no need to make any change in the first place. You took a risk to get yourself a better position.

It is your job to help yourself get back up even after you have tried and failed. And while doing this, make sure that you take yourself back into the exact position you were in before you experienced the failure.

Make sure that you don't idealize your situation. This is really important. To keep yourself protected, you usually view your situation better than the situation actually is. That usually results in not acting at all and this is one big mistake a person can make in failure.

Although problems may resolve on their own sometimes, this is not usually the case. When you fail, the responsibility to get yourself out of the hole rests on you, and you need to be smart to do this. And this requires that you realistically assess your situation.

To go through your failure, you need to understand that no obstacle standing in your way can be bigger than your mission. It is important to have a clear vision of the legacy you want to leave behind in the world and your reason for wanting to fight.

The fuel on the road to success is an emotionally empowered mission and vision. You need to find the emotional why if you decide to continue. Success mantras can be helpful.

Apart from having an emotionally empowered vision, you need to reassure your emotions that what you are doing is the right thing. For this reason, you need to have some early wins after you have failed.

That is why persisting makes sense only if the next few experiments show that you are making progress toward the vision you have. Remember to reward yourself when you make progress. Celebrate every success you achieve after the failure, no matter how small the success may be, because that is the best reassurance that your emotional side needs.

You might find yourself daydreaming about the position that you were in before you failed, and it might even take months to get over the failure. Properly taking care of yourself can stabilize your emotions so you can plan for the next thing to do.

Failure affects your mind as much as it affects your emotional side. For this reason, it is important that you manage your mind well when you are hit by hard times.

Scripting the next moves that you want to make, carefully analyzing the lessons you have learned, and managing your cognitive distortions well will be helpful when it comes to managing your failure successfully.

Cognitive emotions often pile up when you fail. You might change from saying something is not that bad and then start imagining the worst possible outcome of your situation.

Your mind goes crazy without any realistic view of the situation.

Here are the cognitive distortions that are the most common in the act of failure:

- The picture you have of your failure is worse than it actually is. You see it from the point of how people leave you, laugh at you, from the point of social pressure, and how you will remain abandoned and forever alone.
- All you see is your failure. You fail to see the lessons you have learned, the bright spots, and all the new steps you can take.
- You considered your job, relationship, business, or idea everything before you experienced failure, and now you don't see them as anything. The situation seems to suddenly move from a hundred percent to zero percent. But no such thing as a hundred percent failure exists.

It is your responsibility to manage cognitive distortions well and view the situation realistically. You must be aware of your losses as well as your exposure to damage very well. It is also important that you know your next moves, the bright spots, and what the failure has taught you. While doing that, remember to encourage yourself to take action and give yourself a pep talk. Do a careful analysis of the lessons you have learned. Someone might use learning as a cheap excuse for their failures. They might say that they failed but learned some lessons from it. Most times, that is not the case.

You must have a clear understanding of the lessons you have learned. This is known as validated learning. It will help you know the direction to take next.

So, the responsibility you have is to make a list of all that you have learned about yourself, other individuals, the markets, and the entire world. Write down what did not work for you as well as what might work for you.

Analysis paralysis is the last problem to tackle on the rational level. Your mind loves to feel sorry for itself, think about how unfair life has been to you, and drown in self-pity.

When you write a clear action plan for the next steps you will take, it gets you out of the mental paralysis. Your mind won't get stuck on anything if you have a carefully made plan to follow. Understand that you are only using your resources and time wrongly and you are not actually stuck.

On the rational level, the following can happen:

- A piling up of your cognitive distortions. Something you used to enjoy doing and which used to be the most awesome thing for you then turns to nothing and you don't see any positive thing in the situation any longer.
- You do a careful analysis of everything you learned and also the feedback received. You know the next steps to take.
- You have a clear and detailed plan for the next steps to take.

So, how can you handle failure? Sit down and make a clear and detailed plan. After making the plan, make sure that you act immediately.

When you fail and pick yourself back up immediately after the failure, you move yourself into a better position sooner. Nevertheless, it is important that you take time to emotionally process your failure and then come up with a smart plan.

When a person fails, it can be hard to get back up. But having a precise formula for managing failure can help you turn your failure into success.

Let us summarize the steps you can take to manage failure:

- Swing into action immediately. Don't keep waiting for everything to be sorted out before you take any step.
- Do an assessment of the resources that you have left. Assess your emotional enthusiasm, money, time, and so on.
- If you enjoy doing a particular thing but are not making any progress, you can reinvest your resources and make that thing your hobby.
- Don't rush back to the position you were in before you took the risk. Try your best to look for a better position.
- Make sure you clearly see reality as well as the bright spots.
- Be clear about the limit concerning how many experiments you can still use your remaining resources to make.
- Spend time to emotionally process the failure and make sure that you are gentle and compassionate towards yourself as you go through the failure.
- Use your past validated learning as a guide to list all your potential experiments.
- Do an analysis of what failure has taught you, what works for you, and what doesn't work for you.
- If you want to continue trying, you can write down your mission statement and your reason for continuing to try.
- Do a careful scripting of the next steps you will take. Let it include what those steps will be and a breakdown of the resources you will use for them.
- Ensure that the next few experiments result in progress that is measurable and visible.
- Celebrate your small success and give yourself rewards.

- You can consider quitting if you keep trying and there is no progress.

CONCLUSION

Unleashing your inner champion and increasing your odds of victory are what many of us long for. In this book, we discussed how you can unleash this inner champion and become the best version of yourself. Remember that you will encounter obstacles on your way to success. Everyone encounters obstacles, so you are not the only one who faces challenges. Don't bother too much about them. Everyone makes mistakes at one point or the other in their lives, and these mistakes are capable of equipping them to perform better the next time an opportunity shows up.

Everyone knows how overwhelming setbacks can be. Even at that, they are great at motivating people. When an individual who has a fixed mindset makes a mistake, they see it as something bad. This affects their motivation and prevents them from taking risks that will eventually help them. Your goal is to become better and not to be carried away by status. A person with a growth mindset doesn't stay focused on some fairy tale ending where they see themselves as the most talented person. Instead, their focus is on the story and the process.

When a person wins, it can open doors to many more opportunities and successes. Therefore, you need to understand the importance of winning. If the goal you are trying to achieve appears difficult and unachievable, the best thing to do is to take the first step toward achieving that goal. Doing this gets you moving and not stuck in one place. Not everyone becomes successful as they may lack the necessary traits that help people achieve success even when they are faced with many challenges. The person needs to possess the desire to be successful before they can actually achieve success. A person cannot win without this urge, so you need to have the urge to succeed. The individual has to first acknowledge their failures. When he or she embraces them, they will be in a better position to win. Following your ambitions keeps you ahead in the race for success. When you refuse to allow anything to distract you and take your attention away from your goals, you move ahead faster.

Having a growth mindset helps you when the situation gets tough as it increases your resilience and makes you stronger.

If your mindset is fixed, changing it to a growth mindset is important. You need to change how you see failure. Although this may not happen quickly, it is important that you keep practicing until things become different.

One very important key to reaching your potential is getting to know what you want to accomplish in your life. When you have a goal that you are working towards, your mind gets instructions that are clear about what you want to achieve.

If you desire to accomplish something great, the first thing to do is to identify your target. Before a person shoots an arrow, they first identify their target. This means that you need to know where you are headed or else you will not go anywhere. Therefore, you need to identify your purpose in life; this is important.

Making comparisons can hurt you. When you compare yourself with other individuals, it will not benefit you in any way. You should not be competing with other individuals, but yourself alone, and you can do this by performing better than you did the last time. The comparisons will never end if you are used to comparing yourself with other individuals. There will always be something that someone else has that you don't have.

We talked about developing a winner's mindset. This involves harnessing psychological tools as well as certain practices that encourage a victorious and resilient mindset. It does not just involve celebrating the victories. If you want to unleash the champion within, you need to have a winner's mindset.

The mindset of a winner is not just about being the best from the start; it is about pushing boundaries, relentlessly working towards improvement, and coming back stronger after experiencing setbacks. It begins with self-belief, is driven by perseverance, and is made from the triumphs of success and the trials of failure. As you work towards becoming a winner, there are psychological tools that you will need for your journey.

Visualization is one psychological tool that is important. There is power in imagery. Go on a journey in your mind before you hit the track. Visualize every straight path, every turn, and even the victory. Imagine yourself overcoming your challenges and emerging a winner. It is a manifestation of the potential within you and not just a mental rehearsal.

Goal setting is important. Set milestones that you will achieve and ensure that your goals are achievable, measurable, and time-bound. Do your best to celebrate your accomplishments, no matter how small they may be, for they will inspire you to do greater things. Remember that positive affirmations are powerful. The words you speak can bring into existence the reality you seek. So, speak positive words over your life. Use affirmations that resonate with the goals you want to achieve. Tell yourself that you overcome challenges effortlessly and that you are powerful. Positive affirmations remove negative energies from your path.

Don't forget to embrace your failures as we have discussed. You can learn from your failures. Every failure you experience is a lesson in disguise. So, embrace and analyze them. You will understand the lessons and they will help you in the future. Remember, every winner experienced challenges before they eventually became winners.

There will be situations that will be challenging to control, so don't stress too much about them. Just make sure that you stay focused on the things you can control. Your energy should be focused on what you can actually control such as your effort, your preparation, your attitude, and so on.

If you have done all you can and you see that you can't do it on your own, consider getting professional help. The professional will help you come up with strategies that suit your unique challenges, thereby enhancing your resilience and mental stamina.

Winners don't remain in one spot. They keep evolving. So, developing a winner's mindset means that you need to keep evolving. It involves striking a balance between the art of acceptance and the continuous pursuit of excellence. On your journey to a victorious and resilient mindset, every straight, every turn, and every finish line provides you with the opportunity to discover the winner within.

So, are you ready to go into a world where your mindset will help you greatly? Remember that victory is the journey and not just the destination. The champion within is victorious and resilient, so unleash him or her.

Remember that it is the most resilient individual who becomes victorious and not the fastest individual. With the mindset of a winner, every challenge that comes your way is a stepping stone to success.